How to Enjoy Reading Your Bible d

promises. Keith's tips are immediately practical and accessible, whether you have walked with Jesus for thirty years or thirty minutes. If you are a pastor—to adults or students—keep several on hand and start giving them away. Do you want your congregation and your students   and love for the Word? If so, this is the

Bestselling Author, ‹
at Secon

He did it again! Keith Ferrin's tips have helped me dive into the living Word of God and discover how much deeper my relationship with Him can be.

> Dawn Heckert
> Pastor of Children's Ministries
> at Christ Community Church (Leawood, KS)

Never have I come across such a practical, comprehensive book as *How to Enjoy Reading Your Bible*. This book rekindled my passion for reading the Bible.

> Sheryl Nelson
> Director of City Kids School (Kirkland, WA)

Keith Ferrin sits us down at the table of faith and plainly explains how to not simply read the Bible, but to dine on a five-course meal with the Creator of the universe. *How to Enjoy Reading Your Bible* invites us to push the crumbs aside and feast on all God is offering.

> Krista Gilbert
> Mother of Four, Writer, Speaker,
> Connector (Coeur d'Alene, ID)

I have fallen in love with God's Word all over again reading this book. Not only did Keith bring the Word to life for me, but he brought *God* to life for me again! I will be forever grateful.

> Nancy Stephens
> (Parkersburg, WV)

HOW TO
ENJOY
READING
YOUR BIBLE

HOW TO
ENJOY
READING
YOUR BIBLE

KEITH FERRIN

BETHANY HOUSE PUBLISHERS
a division of Baker Publishing Group
Minneapolis, Minnesota

Portions of this text were previously published in *10 Tips for Liking the Bible* (2013)

Published by Bethany House Publishers
11400 Hampshire Avenue South
Bloomington, Minnesota 55438
www.bethanyhouse.com

Bethany House Publishers is a division of
Baker Publishing Group, Grand Rapids, Michigan

Printed in the United States of America

Library of Congress Cataloging-in-Publication Data
Ferrin, Keith.
    How to enjoy reading your Bible / Keith Ferrin.
        pages cm
    Summary: "Speaker Keith Ferrin shows readers how to develop a mindset and approach to reading the Bible that aligns with their own learning styles, helping them to enjoy the Bible, read it more consistently, and apply it to their lives"— Provided by publisher.
        ISBN 978-0-7642-1323-6 (pbk. : alk. paper)
    1. Bible—Reading. I. Title.
BS617.F475 2015
220.071—dc23   2014047138

Cover design by LOOK Design Studio

15 16 17 18 19 20 21   7 6 5 4 3 2 1

To Sarah, Caleb, and Hannah

As you grow, may God's beautiful, mysterious, amazing
story continue to engage you as deeply as it does today.
May you read it, trust it, internalize it, live it . . . and enjoy it!
Love, Dad

Contents

Introduction

I didn't always enjoy the Bible. Not that I disliked it. I didn't even think about enjoying it.

I spent the first twenty years I was a Christian believing that the Bible was true. Still do. Believing the Bible was reliable. Still believe that too. Believing that I should read it more, study it more deeply, and memorize more verses.

But the idea of *enjoying* it didn't even enter the conversation. In fact, I still rarely hear people talk about enjoying the Bible. It is almost as if we think that once we convince people it is true, reliable, and valuable, then they will read it every day, sign up for every Bible study, and memorize it from cover to cover. (Okay, I might have just gone a bit too far.)

If you have ever heard me speak—or read one of my other books—you have heard me tell of the night I began to enjoy the Bible. Yes, I can trace it back to a specific night in the spring of 1993.

A friend told me about an actor named Bruce Kuhn who was coming to his church to "perform" the gospel of Luke.

Bruce had memorized Luke. The whole book. And he got up on stage, quoted it, and acted it out at the same time. No sets. No props. No other actors or actresses.

Honestly, I went out of curiosity. I thought it would be a bit fascinating, but I didn't expect to enjoy it. At least not for almost two hours! But that night, the living Word of God went from being a phrase to a reality. It came alive for me like never before. I sincerely enjoyed it. A lot.

Bruce agreed to have lunch with me the next day. We ended up spending about nine hours together. He challenged me to hang out in a book of the Bible. So I did.

That summer I read Philippians. Every day. All summer. It was the first time I could remember enjoying the Bible consistently for a long period. Thank you, Bruce. I am forever grateful.

That was the summer of 1993. Just under three years later— in March of 1996—I did my first dramatic presentation of the gospel of John. I have spent the better part of the last two decades speaking, writing, and doing everything I can to help people fall in love with God's Word.

What you are about to read is my attempt to boil down the lessons, analogies, ideas, and habits people tell me have been the most helpful for them.

Ten tips. Ten tips you can apply today. Ten tips that are simple to understand. Ten tips that are equally practical for the long-time Bible student or the person who is exploring what the big deal is about this old book.

The Bible *is* a big deal. (Check the all-time bestseller list. It's right at the top.)

Yes, the Bible is true. Yes, it is practical. And yes, it is fun!

My goal is simple: to help you enjoy the Bible. That's it. If you enjoy it, you will read it more. If you enjoy it, you will talk about it. If you enjoy it, you will be more consistent in your time with God. If you enjoy it, you will apply it.

When it comes to the Bible, God never intended you to stop at believing it is true. He also wants you to enjoy it. I do too. So let's get started.

Alongside,
Keith

Tip 1

Remember Why You Are Doing This

Why do you read the Bible?

Take a moment to answer the question before moving on. (Hint: Your answer is really important.)

Whenever I ask this question—especially to a group of people sitting in a church—I typically get replies like this:

"It is an opportunity to know God's will."

"I find encouragement there."

"It is what I am supposed to do."

"It reminds me of what is true."

"It is how I know what God wants me to do."

"It is God's Holy Word."

All of these are true statements. Without a doubt. But once—just once—I would love to hear someone say, "I read it to hang out with God."

After all, isn't that the point? Isn't our time in God's Word primarily about spending time with Him? Being with Him. Knowing Him. Sitting with Him. Learning from Him. Laughing with Him. Hanging out with Him.

One of My Pet Peeves

It has been bugging me for almost twenty years now. I wish it had bugged me for longer. You see, we talk a lot about having a relationship with Jesus. (That's not the part that bugs me.) The part that really gets to me is *when* we talk about having a relationship with Jesus. Or even more specifically—when we *don't* talk about it.

We seem to talk about having a relationship right up to the time when someone actually says, "I'm in." Once someone is in the relationship, we stop talking about it. Odd, don't you think?

All too often the conversation moves pretty quickly to church attendance, volunteering, joining a small group, or reading the Bible to learn about God.

Don't get me wrong. Every one of these is a good and necessary practice. But notice the last three words of the previous paragraph: "learn about God." Isn't the goal of a relationship to know someone, not know *about* them?

In John 14–16, we are given a peek into a very intimate scene. Jesus has shared a meal with the twelve guys He has traveled with for the past three years. One of them has left the meal . . . to betray Jesus. The rest have gone out for a walk. This is His last conversation with them before the worst night and day of His life.

As you might expect, He is talking about things that really matter. Bearing fruit. Staying connected. Enduring suffering. Receiving the Holy Spirit. Having peace. Overcoming the world. (You know . . . big stuff.)

Smack-dab in the middle of this conversation, Jesus says these words:

> I no longer call you servants, because a servant does not know his master's business. Instead, I have called you friends, for everything that I learned from my Father I have made known to you.
>
> John 15:15

Friends. That is what Jesus called them. Not servants. Not partners in business. Not workers or team members or helpers. Friends.

Oh, how our time in the Bible would change if we kept the friendship front and center. If our time in God's Word were primarily relational instead of informational, it would have a significantly higher probability of being transformational!

Is there information in the Bible? *Yes.* Do we learn some things about God in His Word? *Yes.* Does spending time in the Bible lead to a better understanding of God, His will, and His ways? *Yes, yes,* and *yes.*

But the context of that information is the relationship. The umbrella under which all that information sits is the relationship.

So how do we keep the focus on the relationship? I'm glad you asked. Hopefully, these two pictures will help.

Picture One: You, God, and a Cup of Coffee

Imagine that you recently moved to my hometown near Seattle. Some friends introduce us. We find we have a lot in common.

With a desire to get to know each other better, we decide to meet at a local coffee shop once a week before work.

Over the course of the next several weeks, would you and I learn some information about each other? Absolutely. We would most likely learn about our families, what brought you to Seattle, where we grew up, what we do for work, our likes and dislikes, and a wide range of other information.

Now, rewind just a minute and imagine that I show up the first week with a notepad in hand. I sit down, take a sip of coffee, and pick up my pen, and you notice that across the top of the notepad I have written:

82 Things I Need to Know About Joe for Him to Be My Friend

Then I start asking you questions about your family, job, etc. The information I would get would likely be the same information I would learn if we just sat and talked. But how different would it feel? More importantly, what would be the chance of you showing up the next week? Zero.

But don't we do that to God all the time?

We sit down, open our Bibles, grab whatever devotional book we happen to be reading, and begin looking for the "answers" to today's questions. Once we have read the passage and filled in the answers, we must be done. Right?

Doesn't sound very relational to me. Sometimes, I think we walk away from our time with God without ever having been *with* God at all! I wonder how frequently I check off my Had-a-Quiet-Time check box and God is thinking, *Hey, Keith. I'd still like to hang out with you a bit. I'm not finished.*

Ouch.

Picture Two: Playing With God

Some days God wants you to read the Bible and not learn anything.

That may sound strange coming from someone who writes and speaks about studying the Bible. Stick with me for a few more paragraphs and you'll see what I mean.

My wife, Kari, and I have three kids. There are days—or parts of days—when I need to teach my kids something. Other days I need to discipline them. Still others require that I correct them, encourage them, comfort them, or even inspire them to be more than they would otherwise be on their own.

There are also days when we just play catch. Or ride bikes. Or bake cookies. (Okay . . . Kari does the baking with them. I do the quality assurance testing.)

Here's the deal: Those days when we only play together are not less valuable! In many ways, they are more valuable than the days of instruction and correction.

Could you imagine the expressions on the faces of Sarah, Caleb, and Hannah if Kari and I sat them down, looked them in the eyes, and I said, "Your mother and I have decided there is just too much to teach you. Too much you need to be corrected on, instructed about, and yes, even some occasional comforting. Because of this, we have decided we will do no more playing. You three can play with each other and your friends. But we are here to teach, discipline, and comfort you. Off you go."

I can hear the thoughts in your head. *No way. That's insane. How can you give up playing with your kids? That's not a relationship at all.*

Aha. Not a relationship at all.

And yet, so often, that is how I tend to view God. When I pick up the Bible, I am supposed to learn something, get corrected, be inspired, or read some comforting words. Of course there are days when these things happen. But hear this clearly: Sometimes God wants you to pick up His Word and just enjoy the read.

I remember talking to a friend one time who is an actor and director. He told me of a conversation he had years earlier with an older British director. Their conversation was about whether the Bible could hold its own on stage with some of the great theater productions. Not whether it was true, but whether it was *good theater*. After a few minutes, this older man said [insert British accent here]: "Well, you know . . . the Bible is the Word of almighty God. But it also happens to be a jolly good read!"

Amen.

God has much to teach us. We have much to learn. But don't miss the story. It is such a fantastic story! There are heroes, battles, and villains. There are crazy characters, and yes, some dull ones. There are plot twists, mystery, and intrigue. There is humor. Lots of it. I'm not kidding. (Pun intended. Forgive me.)

One of my favorite things about presenting the gospel of John is watching how frequently the audience laughs. They don't expect to, but they do. Every time.

After all, what is the *story* of the Gospels? Aren't they four accounts of thirteen guys on a three-year road trip? Have you ever been on a road trip? Funny stuff happens.

Not only that, but the most serious Bible scholars will tell you that at least a handful of the disciples were teenagers. Have you ever been on a road trip with teenagers?! As someone who spent six years as a youth pastor, I can assure you that laughter is part of the deal.

Even after two decades of telling these stories, it is so easy for me to go back to simply gleaning information from the pages of Scripture rather than being engulfed by the story. I have to constantly remind myself: *It is about the relationship*.

Relationship. Relationship. Relationship.

You *will* be tempted to go back to reading the Bible for information. Don't do it.

Each time you sit down to hang out with God in His Word, get one—or both—of these pictures in your mind: you and God sitting down for a cup of coffee, and God as a daddy who wants to play with you. As your mindset shifts from information to relationship, you will find that you are more likely to be ready on the days when God *does* want to teach you something, inspire you, discipline you, or comfort you.

And you will find that you enjoy the Bible, and the Author, more than ever before.

A Note About the Study Guide

This book comes with a built-in study guide. My prayer is that these chapter-ending discussion questions, additional thoughts, and resource ideas will help you (and hopefully a small group of people you're meeting with) take the next step in applying the tips discussed in the book.

To get the most out of this material:

1. Keep a journal or notepad nearby. Writing down your answers, thoughts, questions, and applications will make your group's conversations much richer.
2. If you prefer, you may also download the study guide questions from www.keithferrin.com/enjoythebiblestudyguide.
3. If you download the study guide, you can electronically "print/send" each chapter's study guide to an online note-keeping program such as OneNote or Evernote. Both are very powerful, super easy, and have free apps for your tablet or phone. They keep everything synchronized so all your notes are always available. Outstanding!

You are probably going to get sick of hearing me say it, but **you need to meet with someone and talk about what you're reading and experiencing.** Preferably four to six people or three to five couples. Weekly works best. Every other week at a minimum. Meet on Skype. Start a Facebook Group or Google Hangout. Something. Just don't try to fly solo.

Now, on to the study guide material for Tip 1 . . .

Study Guide for Tip 1

Remember Why You Are Doing This

Have you lost the *relational* part of your relationship with Jesus? So many people come to know Jesus, and they are so excited, so vibrant, so alive! All too soon the want-to's turn into have-to's, and we get bogged down.

Nowhere is that more true than when it comes to Bible reading. We feel like we should read more. We should know it better. We should memorize more verses. We should enjoy it more than we do. And so many of us practically force ourselves to read instead of spending time with the One who formed us, saved us, redeemed us, restores us, and loves us.

Let's change that. Let's keep the relationship front and center. Let's keep the relationship, well, relational. Oh, and if you're just beginning or exploring a relationship with Jesus, it will be much better if you start relationally and continue relationally. Nourish the want-to's so they don't turn into have-to's.

For the Group

1. When have you felt like you were in a true relationship with Jesus? What were your thoughts, activities, and habits at that time? What changed (if it has)? Describe it.

2. Do you want to be in a true relationship with Jesus? Describe what that would look like for you. Be clear about what you want and need out of your relationship with Jesus. Write it down. (Then put your pen down and talk with Him about it.)

3. How do you feel about the Bible? Do you enjoy it? Did you ever? If so, and you don't now, what changed?

4. Why do you study the Bible? Is your approach more informational or relational?

5. Spend some time sitting in silence, pondering the truth that Jesus calls you "friend." Meditate on John 15:15 for a good five to ten minutes. Then jot down your thoughts.

> I no longer call you servants, because a servant does not know his master's business. Instead, I have called you friends, for everything that I learned from my Father I have made known to you.

> John 15:15

6. What is one practical change you can make to approach the Bible more relationally (e.g., where you read, what chair you sit in, what time of day you read, a way to reduce distractions)?

7. Which of the two pictures (*You, God, and a Cup of Coffee* or *Playing with God*) was most helpful for you? Which is the harder one for you to embrace and live out? Why do you think that is?

8. Recall the story of a British director who once said, "Well, you know . . . the Bible is the Word of almighty God. But it also happens to be a jolly good read." Have you ever thought of the Bible as a "jolly good read"? What are a few stories in the Bible that remind you of that truth?

--- Scripture to Soak In ----------------------------------

- John 1:1–18. Read it in your favorite translation. Then read it in *The Message* by Eugene Peterson. He really brings out the relational tone of the text. (Note: If you don't own a copy of *The Message*, head to www.BibleGateway.com or the YouVersion Bible app. You can read it—and many more translations—there for free.)
- Ephesians 3:12–21
- Romans 5:1–11
- John 10:1–18

SHALL WE PRAY?

Abba Father, Lord Jesus, Great Comforter, the One who created me, knows me, died for me, redeemed me, restores me, and calls me "friend,"

Oh, how I want to know You more. To know Your presence as I read Your Word. To truly meet with You.

I am open to whatever You have for me today. If You want to teach me something, I am here to learn. If You need to correct an error in my thinking or my actions, I am open to Your discipline. If You want to restore something that is broken or needs to be made whole, I admit my brokenness and my need.

And if today Your desire is to simply be together, to laugh, and to enjoy each other's company, I am here, willing and available.

Help me to keep a relational mindset every time I pick up my Bible. Help me to know You more intimately and to follow You more closely. May our relationship be so close and so deep that it transforms every other relationship, motive, thought, and action.

Amen.

Tip 2

Set Your Expectations Really High

Think about the last party you went to. See the people. Taste the food. Hear the conversations, the laughter . . . or the arguments.

If you can, rewind all the way to before you arrived at the party. What was your expectation? Did you expect it to be fun? Did you expect it to be boring? If you went to the party expecting it to be fun, did you have a good time? If you went expecting it to be boring, did you spend most of the evening figuring out a way to duck out early? (Yeah, I've been there.)

Your expectations make a massive difference.

Certainly there are times when an experience wonderfully exceeds (or falls woefully short of) what we expected. Typically, though, that is the exception, not the rule. It is much more common to have our expectation and experience line up pretty closely.

If you go to a movie expecting it to be funny, you will probably find yourself laughing. If you enter a meeting with your boss expecting it to go poorly, the chance of it going well is not too high. If you expect to not like a new food, well . . . ask my three kids how that goes.

When it comes to the Bible, the same rule applies. Your expectations make a massive difference. Most of us expect the Bible to be true, but sadly, we don't expect to like it.

As I wrote in the last chapter, when we read Scripture, we might expect to learn something, be challenged, get corrected, or even receive some comfort. But laugh, cry, or be drawn into the story so deeply that we glance at the clock only to realize we have read longer than we intended? Not usually.

So let me ask you a question . . .

What is your expectation when you open your Bible?

You have expectations when you open your Bible. We all do. They might be high. Or, if you are like many of the people who speak with me after a presentation or send me an email, your expectations are probably pretty low. And if you don't expect to enjoy the Bible, guess what? You won't.

That might sound pretty harsh. But please, please remember, I am someone who spent the first twenty years of my Christian life believing the Bible was true. I just didn't enjoy it very much. Looking back, I am convinced that much of it had to do with my expectations.

It wasn't until I was in my midtwenties—after seeing Bruce Kuhn "perform" the gospel of Luke—that my expectations changed. After that night, I started expecting the Bible to be good. I expected it to be funny, engaging, and enjoyable. Let me tell you, when it comes to my love for God's Word, the last two decades have been much better than the first two!

Take a few minutes and be honest about your own expectations of the Bible. Spend some time talking with God about it. If your expectations are low, tell Him. You are not going to disappoint Him. He already knows.

After sharing your honest expectations with God, let me remind you of something . . .

You can change your expectations.

You don't have to stay where you are. The Bible can be exciting and enjoyable for you. It is possible to have David's words be your own:

> The law of the Lord is perfect, refreshing the soul.
> The statutes of the Lord are trustworthy, making wise the simple.
> The precepts of the Lord are right, giving joy to the heart.
> The commands of the Lord are radiant, giving light to the eyes.
> The fear of the Lord is pure, enduring forever.
> The decrees of the Lord are firm, and all of them are righteous.
> They are more precious than gold, than much pure gold;
> they are sweeter than honey, than honey from the honeycomb.
> Psalm 19:7–10

David loved the Bible. You can too.

However, if your expectations are going to change, you must choose to change them. The Holy Spirit will certainly aid in that process. But He will not force it. After all, if time in God's Word is primarily relational, then both parties have to want to be there. Forcing you to enjoy it makes no sense.

The next time you pick up your Bible, check your expectations first. Pause for a moment and say (maybe even out loud),

God, I am really looking forward to this. I am excited to be with You as I read Your Word. I look forward to hearing Your voice today. I don't know all that You have in store for me, but I eagerly await what You have planned. Use this time to draw me closer to Your heart, to Your joy, to Your peace, to Your hope, and to You.

Set your expectations high. Really high! After all, we are talking about the unfathomable privilege of reading words written by the Author of Life. The One who invented words. The One who created your heart, knows you intimately, and loves you deeply. Then watch what happens.

As with any habit, making the choice to change is the hardest step. The irony is that the more you take time to intentionally set your expectations, the less you will have to be intentional about it. You will find yourself looking forward to the next time you get to read the Bible. And when "have to read the Bible" changes to "get to read the Bible," I guess you won't really need this book anymore!

Study Guide for Tip 2

Set Your Expectations Really High

This one is huge. And the longer I live, the bigger deal I believe it is. I don't remember who said it, but years ago someone said,

> "Our problem is not that we expect too much of God. Our problem is that we expect too little."

I couldn't agree more.

We expect the Bible to be true. We don't expect to enjoy it. We expect to learn from the pages of Scripture. We don't expect to enjoy the learning. We expect to be challenged or corrected. We don't expect to be celebrated and embraced. We expect to think. We don't expect to laugh.

What if you could expect—and experience—all of it?

You can.

For the Group

1. What are your expectations when you open your Bible? (Honest evaluation is going to be really helpful here.)

2. Describe a time when a book, story, psalm, or section of the Bible exceeded your expectations. What was different?

3. If you do expect the Bible to be engaging and enjoyable, have you always felt that way? What helped you make the shift?

4. Reread Psalm 19:7–10. Do you come to the Word with a "David-esque" attitude? Mark this passage in your Bible and read it daily as an "appetizer" to your time in God's Word for the next couple of weeks.

5. What is your reaction (for you personally, your family, your church, and the church at large) when you read the following?

> "Our problem is not that we expect too much of God. Our problem is that we expect too little."

6. What is one or two (. . . or eight) steps you can take to start shifting your expectations when it comes to God and His Word?

----- Scripture to Soak In -----

- Psalm 119:9–16, 97
- Isaiah 40:8
- Luke 8:4–15
- Ephesians 3:20–21
- Hebrews 4:12

SHALL WE PRAY?

Jesus, Living Word,

I confess that my expectations of You and Your Word frequently fall woefully short. I say that Your Word is living, but approach it expecting to be bored or confused.

Today, I need You to change my heart and transform my mind. Grow my desire. Reveal Your heart and Your mind to me as I read Your Word. Help me see the life— Your life—contained on the pages of my Bible. Grow my expectations. Start today. And may my expectations of You and Your Word grow stronger and deeper day after day after day.

Amen.

Tip 3

Have a Strategy

There is one question I have asked hundreds of times to thousands of people. The response is *always* the same. Sighs are heavy. Eyes are rolled. Hands are raised. The question?

Is there anyone here who struggles with their
mind wandering when they read the Bible?

Excuse me, did you just let out a heavy sigh?

I meet very few people who *don't* struggle with this. The Wandering Mind is something I have battled against for as long as I can remember. Not just when I was young. Throughout my teens, into my twenties and beyond, the struggle has been present on a daily basis.

One morning it all came to a head. I was so frustrated. I had been a Christian for twenty-five years. I had already internalized

Philippians, the gospel of John, and 2 Timothy. I had been doing dramatic presentations of the gospel of John for a couple of years. I knew how awesome the Bible could be. And yet, I couldn't get more than two or three paragraphs into the Bible without my mind drifting off into space. I simply could not focus. And I was mad. This is the conversation I had with God after closing my Bible in frustration.

Me: "God . . . What is wrong with me? Why can't I focus? I love You. I love Your Word. I know it is alive. But it doesn't feel alive. Why is it that I can read a novel for two hours without having my mind drift at all, but I can't read two paragraphs of the Bible without thinking of a million different things?"

God: "Excuse me. Can I talk now?"

Me: "Er . . . um . . . okay . . ."

The following dream/analogy/vision popped into my head. (I know this might be scary, but go with me into my brain.)

I was a running back on a football team. My team was on the twenty-yard line. Eighty yards to go. My number was called. I was getting the ball.

I had prepared. I had practiced. I was in shape. I had studied the playbook. I knew where the hole was going to be and what blockers to follow. And I had done that all-important task of "visualizing" the end zone. I could already hear the crowd cheering.

The quarterback handed me the ball and off I went. Three yards . . . on my way . . . ten yards . . . wahoo! . . . twenty-two yards. . . . BLAM! Flat on my back.

"Hmm . . . Why am I not in the end zone? I visualized the end zone. I want to be in the end zone. Why am I not in the end zone?"

A teammate came over to help me up and heard me mumbling those questions to myself. He simply responded, "Hey, man. It might have something to do with the guys playing defense."

Did you catch that? I had never even thought about it. Every time you and I sit down to read our Bibles, there is someone playing defense. Someone who is actively trying to make sure we don't enjoy it. Someone who is throwing distractions our way. And the "defense" starts early. It starts before you even pick up your Bible. Have you ever heard any of these?

"You don't have time to read the Bible."
"It won't make a difference anyway."
"There are more important things to do."
"You need that extra thirty minutes of sleep way more than you need time with God."

And it continues as we read. Distractions. Random thoughts. Even important things that need to be thought about but could wait till later.

For years, every time I would get distracted, I would simply blame myself. Thoughts like, *Why can't I focus? Why don't I enjoy the Bible? I don't think I'll ever get better at this. I should just quit.* Where do those thoughts sound like they come from? Anyone who has ever played sports will tell you that as soon as you can get the other team down on themselves, your work is done. Game over.

Bottom line: We need a strategy for beating the defense. By far, the best strategy is prayer.

This is not a simple two-second "help me focus" prayer. This is strategic prayer. In fact, there are three specific times when prayer will help you "beat the defense."

1. Pray before you ever open your Bible.

I don't encourage you to start with prayer because it is the "Christian" thing to do. I put it first because it is truly the most important. Going back to Tip 1, if we are going to shift from informational Bible study to relational Bible study, it is probably not a bad idea to begin by chatting with God.

There are three prayers I pray before I ever start reading. Each helps get me in the right mindset as I prepare to read.

"God, thank You for Your Living Word."

It is easier to focus on something we are grateful for, as opposed to something we feel obligated to. "God, thank You for Your Living Word" is a simple prayer, but an important one nonetheless.

The God of the universe has given you His Word. He is talking with you. He wrote these words centuries ago—with you in mind! This isn't simply a textbook to be studied. It is a poem, a letter, a novel, a guidebook, a biography, and an autobiography . . . all rolled up together. And it is for you. Starting with a thankful heart will keep you engaged as you read.

"God, what do You want to do today?"

As you have likely gathered by now, time in God's Word is primarily a relational activity—not an informational one. For many of us, we have spent years studying the Bible informationally. It is now a habit to approach the Bible with a mindset that says, *God, what do You want to teach me today?*

What if God doesn't want to teach you anything? What if He just wants to hang out with you? What if he wants to encourage you, comfort you, or simply remind you that He has been in relationships with a lot of messy people (just like you and me) for a very long time? We have already explored this, but it bears repeating: Some days God most certainly will want to teach you something. Just not every day. If you have either been a parent or had parents, you know this intuitively. Some days my dad taught me stuff. Then there were days when we just played catch. Both were necessary.

Asking this question helps us approach our time in the Bible conversationally. After all, would you be able to stay focused on a conversation with a friend who only wanted to teach you things every time you got together? You would quickly get bored. Then you would stop getting together. Sounds like my pattern of Bible reading for the first twenty years.

"God, help me focus."

Sounds simple, doesn't it? But doesn't asking God to help you focus make sense? To continue the football analogy from earlier, if someone is playing defense, aren't we better off with blockers? So frequently we forget that God has angels prepared to help us.

> Are not all angels ministering spirits sent to serve those who will inherit salvation?
>
> Hebrews 1:14

No running back would ever step on the field without bringing his teammates along. If the enemy is actively trying to make sure that we don't enjoy our time in God's Word, why would we ever try to fight that fight on our own? What chance do we stand? But if God's angels are blocking for us, that's another story.

Next time you reach for your Bible, pause for a few minutes and pray these three prayers. You will be surprised how much easier it is to focus—and how much more you enjoy it.

2. Pause to pray while you are reading.

Again—this is not rocket science—but pausing to pray is so frequently left out.

Here is a common scenario: I begin reading. Two paragraphs in, and my mind is off who-knows-where. I tell myself, "Okay, Keith. You are going to focus. You can do it. Focus." This typically works for about two more paragraphs. About the third time I have this conversation with myself, I am pretty frustrated. Might even put the Bible down and chalk this one up to a bad day of time in God's Word. I'll try again tomorrow.

Really? A "bad day"?

Back to the running-back analogy. I have never seen a running back get tackled a few times and then simply walk off midway through the first quarter and chalk it up to a "bad day" on the field. He might be frustrated. He certainly didn't want to get tackled.

What I usually see is a running back on the sidelines, talking with the coach. Making plans for the next time he goes out on the field. New strategies for beating the defense. Maybe even a quick pep talk. This all takes place *in the middle of the game*.

Now, when I find my mind wandering, I stop and talk to the Coach. When I do, I am reminded of three truths.

The Coach is on my side.

I am not alone in this. You are not alone in this. God is pulling for you. He is on your side. He wants your time in His Word to be beneficial and enjoyable. Knowing that God is for you—instead of disappointed in you—is an enormous encouragement as you begin reading again.

The Coach knows how to beat the defense.

God has been at this a long time. He knows all of the enemy's tricks. He is not surprised by any of it. When we pause to talk to God and share our frustrations and ask for help, He is more than happy to give it . . . without blame or shame. As the apostle James wrote, "If any of you lacks wisdom, you should ask God, who gives generously to all without finding fault, and it will be given to you" (1:5). He will remind us of His presence. He will send "blockers" to keep distractions away.

The Coach sometimes just wants to chat.

Most of the time, my prayer in the middle of reading is quite short—often less than a minute. But there are times when I never get back to my Bible reading. I spend time talking with God. And listening to God (arguably more important than the talking part). Even when my intention is to spend thirty to forty-five minutes reading the Bible, if I end up reading for five minutes and chatting with God the rest of the time, that is not time poorly spent.

Before moving on, I want to make it clear that my mind still wanders sometimes—even right after I have been talking with the Coach. That is when I pause, chat with the Coach again, and get back at it. After all, I have yet to meet a running back who figured out a way to never get tackled. Even so, they always want to get back in the game.

3. Pray after you close your Bible.

This may seem like an odd strategy when the goal is to keep your mind from wandering *while* you are reading the Bible. Maybe this will help . . .

Have you ever had one of those projects at work—or classes in school—where you couldn't stop thinking about it when you were away from it? When you returned, how focused were you? Did you have to work at keeping your mind from wandering? Probably not.

> The more you think about something
> while you are away from it, the easier
> it is to focus when you return.

So often we set aside time to read or pray. But that's just it. We "set aside" time to read or pray. It is designated time, not a practice that permeates our lives. Seems I read something somewhere about praying continually (see 1 Thessalonians 5:16–18).

If we want to be able to focus while we read, we have got to be in conversation with God when we are *not reading*. Those conversations will develop our hunger for the Word—a longing to get back to the Word—to continue the conversation as we read.

It is essential to spend some time in prayer immediately after reading the Bible. As I am wrapping up my time in the Word, I pray a prayer similar to this:

> *Lord Jesus, help me remember what I have read here this morning. Let's talk about this again throughout the day. Bring it to my mind as I have periods of downtime— when I'm driving my car, eating my lunch, or brushing*

my teeth. Remind me of Your Word as I face situations where Your Word would bring needed comfort, a helpful reminder, valuable instruction, or even necessary correction. Let your Word saturate my thoughts and attitudes.

It is also crucial to pray at any and every other time. I know, I know. Sounds like a good Sunday school answer. But how often do we ignore the times when God actually answers the first prayer? He brings something to mind and we don't engage in the conversation He is starting. We will gladly pick up our cell phone for anyone who happens to call at any random time. But when God calls? Too busy. *He couldn't really be talking to me. I am imagining this.*

What would happen if we prayed that God would talk to us throughout the day, expected that He would, and then engaged in the conversations when He did? Those conversations would become easier, more frequent, more enjoyable, and more fruitful. We would become shaped by them. We would look forward to them.

And when we returned to the Bible? We wouldn't struggle as much with our wandering mind, because we would anticipate meeting Jesus there. And indeed we would meet Him.

Pray before reading your Bible. Pray in the middle. Pray after. It might sound simple, but in this case, simple is exactly what is needed most.

Study Guide for Tip 3

Have a Strategy

Our minds wander. It is frustrating. You can either simmer in the frustration or move forward with a strategy. (I highly recommend the latter.)

So often we completely ignore the fact that there is someone "playing defense." I have heard it said (from many people on many occasions) that

> There are two mistakes we commonly make
> when it comes to the devil: We either blame
> him for everything or pretend he doesn't exist.

Either mistake moves us no further toward enjoying the Bible or staying focused while we read. The analogy of the running back is—without a doubt—the analogy people tell me has helped them the most. Year after year people tell me they get frustrated, remember someone is playing defense, and picture the running back jumping up and asking the coach to put him in again.

Your mind will wander. Sometimes only two minutes into your reading. But remember there is a defense. Remember your Coach. Remember your strategy. And get back in the game.

For the Group

1. On a scale of 1 to 10 (with 1 being "I can't get through a verse" and 10 being "I can typically read for about an hour"), how badly does your mind wander?

2. What was your initial reaction to the running-back analogy? Had you ever thought that there was "someone playing defense"?

3. Do you have (or have you ever had) a strategy for "beating the defense"? What has helped in the past?

4. Which of the three "before you read" prayers do you think will be most helpful for you? Jot down your answer. Now pray these prayers before you read for the next week. Write down your thoughts again at the end of the week. You can also use this prayer:

> *I confess, Lord, that my mind drifts when I want to focus. My thoughts turn to other things when they should be centered on You. My desire is to focus on You, engage with You, hear from You, and know You more as I read Your Word. Protect my mind. Guard me from the attacks of the enemy. Help me be fully present as I read today. Amen.*

5. Do you ever stop and "talk with the Coach" in the middle of your Bible reading? Write down your reaction to these three statements:

- The Coach is on my side.
- The Coach knows how to beat the defense.
- The Coach sometimes just wants to chat.

6. For the next week, finish your Bible reading by praying the prayer I suggested a few pages earlier for after you close your Bible. Then, set a Bible-reading reminder on your phone or computer that simply says "Listen. Expect. Obey." Write down your experience here.

―― Scripture to Soak In ―――――――――――――――――――――

- Philippians 4:4–9
- Romans 12:1–2
- 1 Peter 5:8–11

SHALL WE PRAY?

Father God, my great Protector and Defender,
Help me remember what I have read in Your Word.
Let's talk about this again. Bring it to my mind as I have periods of downtime—when I'm driving my car, eating my lunch, or brushing my teeth. Remind me of Your Word as I face situations where Your Word would bring needed comfort, a helpful reminder, valuable instruction, or even necessary correction. Let your Word saturate my thoughts and attitudes.
Amen.

Tip 4

Watch the Whole Movie

I love movies. And I am not really picky. Action movies. *Of course.* Comedies. *Who doesn't like them?* Intense thrillers? *The more twists the better.* Cheesy romantic comedies. *Guilty.*

Now, picture this scene. Kari and I have invited you and a few other friends over to watch a movie. You find a cozy spot on the couch. Your feet land on the ottoman only moments before your hand lands in the popcorn bowl. You grin as you realize your fingertips are now coated with that heavenly blend of butter and salt. I push *Play* and a couple of minutes later, the opening credits dissolve into Scene One. As the scene comes to a close, I push *Pause* and say, "Let's discuss this before watching scene two." You politely participate in the awkward conversation and a few minutes later, I push *Play*. At the end of scene two, I do it again. And again after scene three. Watch . . . pause . . . discuss. Watch . . . pause . . . discuss.

How much would you enjoy that evening? Actually, since we are pausing to discuss every scene, watching the movie will need to be spread out over the next eight Friday nights. Two months will pass before the final credits roll.

This might sound completely absurd, but don't we do the very same thing to the Bible all the time? We decide we are going to study a book of the Bible, so we break it down into small pieces. We look at one piece, discuss it, and then do the same with the next piece. We never sit down and just read it.

To enjoy the Bible, read *more* of it.

Stop for a second and think of your favorite novelist. This author has just come out with a new book. You pick up a copy and immediately dive in. But wait a second. What if I said you could read only one page a day? How much would you enjoy that book? Take this one step further. What if you could read only a couple of paragraphs each day? Would it even be possible to get through it? Not likely.

We wouldn't even think about reading a novel that way. And yet, when I ask people how they read the Bible, by far the most common answers I get are:

"I read a chapter a day."

"I read whatever is in my devotional."

Do you realize that the average chapter of the Bible takes less than four minutes to read? The average section of Scripture in a devotional book takes about thirty seconds! Can you think of anything that you can read for thirty seconds to four minutes a day and truly enjoy? (Okay . . . maybe the comics, but I can't think of anything else.)

Not only that, it simply doesn't make sense to read only a little at a time. I will use the book of Philippians to show what I mean.

It probably wouldn't be a huge revelation if I told you that Philippians is a four-chapter letter written by the apostle Paul to the church in Philippi. Now, imagine that you went out to your mailbox and tucked in the middle of the pizza coupons, bills, and credit card offers was an envelope with your name handwritten on the outside. In the corner was the name of someone you love whom you hadn't seen in a few years. Inside you find a four-page handwritten letter. The letter starts out,

Dear Elizabeth, I thank my God every time I remember you. Every time I pray for you, I pray with joy.

Would you read page one and say, "That is enough for today. I better save page two for tomorrow. Four days from now, I'll finish this up"?

Not a chance. You would read it, realize you are still standing by your mailbox, go inside, and read it again! So why don't we do that with Philippians? That's how Philippians starts. It is a letter. A letter from someone who loves and misses his friends. A letter about joy in the midst of struggle. A letter written with a deep sense of gratitude and partnership. How often we miss these sorts of things because we are too busy "studying" the Bible.

Please, please don't hear what I am not saying. I am not saying you should never study a chapter or a paragraph, or even meditate on a single word or phrase. What I am saying is that detailed study is not the place to start. Talking about a single scene, character, or plot twist in a movie is valuable and enjoyable. But only after you have seen the movie. (We will explore this in a bit more detail in Tip 9.)

Next time you pick up your Bible, sit down and read a whole book. More than half of the sixty-six books in the Bible can be read in less than thirty minutes. Pick one of those. Try Philippians, 2 Timothy, James, or 1 Peter. Reading at an average the-way-you-would-talk pace, you will finish in less than twenty minutes. And you will reap some fantastic benefits.

You will easily enter the story.

Give it a try. Reading more will trigger something in your brain. You will start to see the characters, hear their voices, and visualize the events. It won't take a lot of extra effort. It will just happen.

Here's the proof. Remember the last time you saw a movie after reading the book on which the movie was based? What was your reaction? If you are anything like me, you probably had to force yourself to keep from yelling at the screen:

Hey! Did the casting director even read the book? She was taller. He had darker hair. They lived in San Francisco, not San Diego!

Now, try to recall the last time you started a novel but got pulled away after only a couple of pages. What did you do when you returned to the book? I bet you didn't start on page 3. Of course not. You started at the beginning, because the last time you never got into it.

The same can—and will—happen with the Bible. When we read more of it, we easily get into it. When we read little bits, we don't. It is as simple as that.

You will remember what you read.

Have you ever read the Bible in the morning, gone on with the rest of your day, and then couldn't remember what you read when someone asked you about it later in the day? You remember sitting down with your Bible and your cup of coffee. You remember what chair you sat in. You remember what time it was when you started and ended. But no matter how hard you try, you can't remember *what* you read. Ugh. Talk about frustrating!

When you read a whole book of the Bible—or a large chunk of a longer book—you will be tapping into how your brain naturally and easily learns anything. Yes . . . *anything*. Our brains learn from the big to the small. The reverse is also true. Our brains do not learn easily from the small to the big. Looking at details first never leads to long-term memory. Put another way:

Our brains learn in the context of story.

Try this. Think of something you know really well. Something you could explain in broad terms or great detail. It might be your favorite sport. Maybe some aspect of your job. Could be music or plumbing or oceanography or painting or entering dog shows.

Got it? Now, how did you first learn about it? Did someone sit you down and teach you one tiny detail? Or did they sit with you and watch a game, take you to a concert, or visit an aquarium?

One example I frequently use is soccer. While soccer is a growing sport in the United States, it certainly is nowhere near as popular as football, basketball, or baseball. Typically, when I ask an audience how many people have played a lot of soccer, about 5 to 10 percent of hands will go up.

If I sat down with the folks who raised their hands, we could jump into a detailed conversation about the strategy of a flat defense versus an arced defense versus a diamond defense. In competitive soccer, this is an important concept to understand and know when to apply.

That said, there is a 90 to 95 percent chance that the words of that last paragraph sounded to you like the adults in a Peanuts cartoon. *Wah, wah wah wah* . . .

It would be much better for me to explain soccer by starting with, "There are eleven guys on one side. Eleven guys on the other. Get the ball in the net on the opposite end of the field. By the way—no hands!" After that, we could break it down to offense, midfielders, defense, and goalies. Much, much later, we could have detailed conversations about the techniques and strategies of each. Is the detail important? *Yes.* Is it the starting point? *No way.*

The same holds true with the Bible. When you start by looking at one paragraph or one chapter, you are trying to force your brain to take in the content in a way that it wasn't designed to take it in. When you "watch the movie," you will remember it. The story will stick. The context will be set as a foundation. After that foundation has been laid, it will always be present, making the detailed study a deeper discussion of a story you already know.

What about the longer books?

I get this question all the time. As I mentioned earlier, a majority of the sixty-six books of the Bible can be read in less than thirty minutes. That still leaves twenty-five to thirty books that can't be read in one sitting. Unless you have four hours every day, you are not going to be able to apply this when you study Genesis. In cases like these, here is what I recommend:

Read for an amount of time . . .
not an amount of chapters.

Reading for an amount of time puts you in a different mindset than reading an amount of chapters. For example, if you decide to read six chapters, your mindset at the end of each chapter will be, "I have five/four/three more chapters to get through." If you instead set aside thirty minutes to read (more than enough time for six chapters), your mindset will shift to, "I still get to read for fifteen more minutes." That shift from "get through" to "get to" is huge.

So, decide beforehand how much time you have. When I ask, most people tell me they have fifteen, twenty, or thirty minutes. Let's take the middle time—twenty minutes—and apply that to reading a long book: the gospel of John.

If you read at an average pace, the gospel of John takes just about two hours. Since it has twenty-one chapters, if I read using the Chapter-a-Day method, it will take me three weeks. (And that's if I never miss a day!) However, if I simply decide to read for twenty minutes each day, I will read the whole book three-and-a-half times in that same three-week period.

How much more will I remember if I go with the second option? Not only that, but how much more will I *enjoy it*?

I have said it before, but it is too important not to repeat: Our brains learn naturally and easily in the context of story. The only way we are going to understand the Story, remember the Story, and enjoy the Story is by reading the Story. The whole thing. In one sitting whenever possible.

Study Guide for Tip 4

Watch the Whole Movie

Of all the tips in this book, this one feels the most like common sense to me. Of course, it never even crossed my mind to do it until I had already been walking with Jesus for two decades! I guess what they say is true: Common sense isn't common until you know it.

It seems like every sermon, small group, curriculum, and Bible study starts with a little piece of Scripture. Then we look at the next little piece. Then the next.

Even with the ones that talk about the "big picture," it seems like so few ever hang out in the big picture. You know, staying in the overarching story until you can actually tell someone the overarching story. We don't do that. We skim it once. Then we dive in to the details.

Once I started reading whole books, my love for God's Word—and remembrance of what I read—skyrocketed. I pray the same happens for you.

—— For the Group ————————————————————

1. This chapter started with a picture of a group of people getting together and watching a movie, but pausing after each scene to discuss it. How painful would this be? What did it make you think about your approach to Bible studies?

2. When was the first time you read a whole book of the Bible in one sitting (if you have)? What was your experience?

3. Pick a short book from the Bible—Philippians, 2 Timothy, James, or 1 Peter—and read it in one sitting. (Tip 6 will discuss the benefits of reading Scripture out loud.) Write down your observations. What was the author's tone? What stood out to you? What was confusing? What was clarified?

4. What is something you know really well (a sport, a hobby, an author, politics, etc.)? How did you learn about it? What is your first memory of it? Describe the process of becoming an "expert" next time you're together as a group.

5. Do you agree or disagree with this statement: "*Our brains learn in the context of story*"? How have you found this to be true (or untrue)?

6. Pick a longer book of the Bible like Genesis or one of the Gospels. Set aside an amount of time (no less than fifteen minutes). Set a timer and just read until it goes off. Finish the chapter, bookmark the page, and do the same thing the next day. Jot down your thoughts and discuss your experience with the group. It's a great idea to have everyone in the group do this exercise on the same week with the same book.

— Scripture to Soak In ——————————————

- Short book—Philippians, 2 Timothy, James, or 1 Peter
- Longer book—Genesis, Matthew, Mark, Luke, or John

SHALL WE PRAY?

Lord God, the Inventor of Stories,

Help me to truly enter into Your story today—to not only see with my mind's eye, but also hear with my mind's ear, smell with my mind's nose, feel with my mind's skin, and taste with my mind's mouth.

Show me the big picture. The overarching themes. The lessons and truths that span several pages, not just several words or sentences. May my appreciation of Your story prepare me for the times when I will study deeply and meditate on a word, verse, or paragraph.

Amen.

Tip 5

Learn From Your Shampoo Bottle

A story is told of a CEO who wanted to foster creativity throughout his toiletries company. He sent out a memo inviting anyone at any level in the company to submit ideas for how to increase sales. Any employee whose idea showed demonstrable, positive impact would receive a small percentage of the profits.

Ideas came in. Some good. Some less than good. The CEO was intrigued when one of the factory workers came in and simply said, "I have an idea that will cost almost nothing and will increase sales by 40 to 70 percent." The CEO raised a disbelieving eyebrow and asked the man to elaborate. He simply picked up a shampoo bottle, pointed at the directions, and said, "Add the word 'repeat.' Lather. Rinse. Repeat."

I have searched, but haven't been able to prove—or disprove—the veracity of this story. (But I sure hope it's true.) A version of it has made its way into at least one novel, *The Plagiarist* by Benjamin Cheever. Either way, look on the back of almost any shampoo bottle and you will see it: *Repeat*.

We will benefit greatly if we apply the same principle to Bible reading. In the last tip, I made the argument that reading whole books will help you remember what you read. Let's keep that "remember" theme going.

What gets repeated gets remembered.

We don't need to spend a long time on this one because you intuitively—and experientially—know it to be true. Let me ask you:

Have you ever been listening to the radio and had a song come on you hadn't heard in over a decade? Were you singing along by the second line?

Do you recall any old addresses or phone numbers?

Can you finish any of these sentences?

- M&M's: *Melts in your mouth, not* _____.
- Rolaids: *How do you spell* _____?
- Dodge: *Dodge trucks are* _____ *tough*.
- Smith Barney: *They make money the old-fashioned way. They* _____.
- The Energizer bunny: *He keeps* _____ *and* _____ *and* _____.

If you're a parent, do you have any VeggieTales songs in your head that you wish would go away? (Even though your kids are now in college!)

Not too long ago, I was speaking to the student body at Moody Bible Institute in Chicago. In an effort to make this same point, I simply said, "Finish this sentence: 'Hello. My name is Inigo Montoya . . .'" The point was made when 1,500 college students yelled back: ". . . you killed my father. Prepare to die!" (Sidenote: If you have never seen the 1987 film *The Princess Bride*, you owe it to yourself to watch it. Soon. Life-changing. Not *Schindler's List* life-changing. More like silly-and-super-funny-with-heaps-of-quotable-lines life-changing.) I asked how many had ever *tried* to memorize that line. Of course, no one raised a hand. (One class clown up in the balcony shouted out, but I haven't been able to track him down.) The students didn't need to memorize it. In the movie, he says it six times. Most of those students have seen the whole movie at least six times. After hearing it thirty-six times, it was in there!

One last thing before we move on to the next benefit. When these students shouted the ending of the movie line, they used an accent like Inigo's! A few of them even shouted out some other lines. When I asked them if they could picture Inigo chasing the six-fingered man through the castle, there was laughter and hoots of affirmation.

Why? Because Tip 4 and this tip go hand in hand.

I ended the last chapter by saying that our brains learn naturally and easily in the context of story. The *context* is story, but the *process* is repetition. We learn in the context of story by the process of repetition.

Repetition will lead to more frequent conversations with God.

We began this whole journey together by remembering that Bible reading is about the relationship. This might sound obvious, but the relationship doesn't end when you close your Bible. Ideally, your time in God's Word should foster conversations with God throughout the day. This will happen if repetition is built in to your Bible reading.

When you "soak" in the same section of Scripture for days— or weeks—at a time, God will weave it in and through your daily life. He will bring to mind an encouraging passage when frustration or discouragement rears its head. At just the right moment, when you don't know what to say to a friend, God will remind you of the promise you read that morning. When your eyes and mind go where they shouldn't go, He will gently—or not so gently—shake you and remind you where your focus should be.

This has truly been one of the most beneficial and enjoyable changes I have seen in my own Bible reading over the last twenty years. The Bible is no longer just something I do early in the morning. It is part of a conversation that starts early in the morning and continues throughout the day. That didn't happen until I committed to staying with one book, story, or psalm—sometimes for weeks at a time.

Repetition is the precursor to enjoying detailed study.

I understand that not everyone is a sports fan, but allow me to revisit the soccer analogy for a couple of paragraphs. I truly enjoy talking about the intricacies of soccer. I love exploring ideas for teaching new skills and strategies to the girls on my daughter's team (which I have coached for the last several years). I have fun talking with fellow fans of Seattle's professional team, the Sounders FC, about the fantastic plays and the failed attempts from the previous match.

The same is not true for every sport or even every soccer team. I don't have a basic knowledge of every sport. I haven't watched every professional soccer team. I am not familiar with their strengths, weaknesses, players, or coaches. If I acquired a basic knowledge of a sport or team, then I would be ready to have a more detailed conversation.

For many of us, we put detailed study of the Bible *ahead* of general understanding. Then we wonder why we don't enjoy it more. We try to figure out what Philippians 4:13 means without being able to say what the book of Philippians is about. We have discussions about what Paul meant when he said, "I have fought the good fight, I have finished the race, I have kept the faith" (2 Timothy 4:7). Still, many of us don't realize that Paul wrote those words from death row, just weeks or months before he was executed. If someone asked us, "What is 2 Timothy about?" all we could offer would be a blank stare.

There is a solution, however: read, reread, repeat. You might not think you could ever love meditating on a single paragraph or doing a word study. If either of those is your starting point, I would agree with you. But if you read the book or section over and over until it was a part of you first? I guarantee you that your deeper study would be much more enjoyable.

I imagine that you enjoy having deep conversations with friends you know well. I bet you can easily remember a multi-hour conversation over coffee. It probably isn't a difficult task to recall a time when a small group of friends shared struggles, prayed for each other, and even wept with each other.

Now, imagine that someone you didn't know tried to have one of those conversations with you—the first time you met! Talk about awkward. Frankly, it would be inappropriate. It isn't time to go that deep. Not yet. But once you know each other—once you have history, once you can carry that relational history into the conversation—then it is time. That is when deep, intimate conversation becomes not only appropriate, but wonderful.

The same is true with the Bible. After you have repeatedly read a section, deep study becomes like that intimate conversation. The whole story stays with you. You don't forget the big picture just because you are focusing on a small section. That's like saying you would forget what a movie is about because you are having a conversation about a single scene. That makes no sense. Having a conversation about a single scene is actually enjoyable—provided you have seen the movie!

How many times should I read and reread?

The short answer is Until you know it. The slightly longer answer is It depends on how long a book is, what genre it is, and how well you want to know it.

For shorter books that I am planning to study deeply and internalize, my general rule is "thirty times in thirty days." Take a short book—like Philippians or 2 Timothy—and read it every day for a month. Watch what happens. After a week, you will notice that you simply *feel* differently about it than you did before. You will start to see the characters as real people. You will picture them and hear their voices. After a month, you will be more than ready to dive in deeper. (More on the day-by-day process in Tip 9.)

With Psalms and Proverbs, I like to take one chapter at a time instead of reading the whole book. In my opinion, the more poetic genres are meant to be read and experienced more than picked apart. My favorite thing to do is to take a psalm and simply read it each morning and evening for a few days or a week. Then go on to the next one. You can certainly do the same thing with Proverbs. I have met many people who read one chapter in Proverbs a day. Since there are thirty-one, they end up reading the whole book a dozen times every year. To read a longer book thirty times would take quite a while. I don't have a set rule for longer books. My approach really goes back to something Bruce Kuhn said to me in 1993, the day after I first saw him present the gospel of Luke. We were having lunch, and I asked him how he went about memorizing (I hadn't started using the word *internalizing* yet) the whole gospel of Luke. He simply said:

> "Memorize the story first. Then use the words on the page to tell the story."

Those words have stuck with me for twenty years now. Today I give you the same advice: Memorize the story first. With a longer book—like Genesis or one of the gospels—read it until you know the story. Read it until you could walk someone through the book without leaving any of the stories out. Read it until the story, the rhythm, and the flow become a part of you. At that point, you will *want* to go deeper. So dive in.

Study Guide for Tip 5

Learn From Your Shampoo Bottle

Read it. Reread it. Then read it again.

Not profound. But it works. When people ask me to summarize my process for internalization, my answer is always the same:

> Read it over and over again until you can tell
> the story in your own words without leaving
> out many of the details. Once you can say
> it in your own words, learning the words on
> the page isn't nearly as hard as you think.

This is a slight expansion of something Bruce Kuhn told me the day after I first saw him present the gospel of Luke. As you may recall, I had asked him how he learned the whole gospel and he said, "Memorize the story first. Then use the words on the page to tell the story."

Read it. Reread it. Then read it again. (Sorry if I'm repeating myself. Wink.)

— For the Group —

1. Think of anything you do or know well. Anything you do without thinking. Anything you know inside and out. How many times have you done it? How many times have you studied it or read about it?

2. Pick a parable or short psalm. Simply read it—out loud— every morning and/or evening for a week. At the end of the week, just try to say it. How much of it did you have down word for word? Did you ever find yourself thinking about it during the day? Write about the experience.

3. The amount of repetition it takes to cement something in your mind will vary depending on the person. If there is a section of the Bible you want to internalize word for word, try practicing at different times of the day. Note what time(s) works best for you.

4. Ask a friend if he or she would read and internalize the same passage(s) as you. When you get together, start by *telling* each other the story. Once you've got the story down, then move on to telling the story by using the words of Scripture.

5. Read and reread a short book of the Bible for at least a week. What conversations did you have with God? How often did the themes—or specific verses—come to mind?

6. This will take a little longer, but after you have read a short book of the Bible enough that you know the big picture, take some time to do a deeper study. On each day, focus on a couple of paragraphs or even a single verse. Use this space to note how different the deeper study feels from when you've done verse-by-verse studies in the past.

—— Scripture to Soak In ——————————————

- Joshua 1:7–9
- Short book—Philippians, 2 Timothy, Colossians, or 1 Peter
- Parables—Matthew 13; 18; 20–22; 24–25; Mark 4; 12–13; Luke 12–19. This isn't a complete list, but it is a good start.
- Psalms—8; 16; 19; 23; 42; 63; 90; 91; 92; 103

SHALL WE PRAY?

Heavenly Father, the Great Storyteller, my Teacher,
   Help me to be so immersed in Your Word that it never leaves me. Help me read it, learn it, know it, internalize it, and carry it with me throughout the day. Bring it to mind that I might have fellowship with You throughout the day.
   I need Your guidance, Your wisdom, Your comfort, Your truth, and Your presence. I need You. May Your Word be so present in my heart and mind that Your Holy Spirit transforms me to be more like Your Son, Jesus.
   Amen.

Tip 6

Raise Your Voice

Back in Tip 3, I said that prayer is the number one strategy for "beating the defense." While prayer is the top strategy, it isn't the only strategy. Something else has become absolutely essential for me. To be completely transparent, I discovered it by accident. I don't remember anyone ever teaching it to me. I don't remember reading about it in a book on Bible study or learning it in a class. And yet, I use it every day.

Read out loud.

The beauty of reading out loud is that it isn't an additional step in the Bible study process. It is not something you have to add on. Other than the fact that you probably read a little more slowly when you read out loud, it doesn't take extra time. Since the goal is *enjoying* the Bible—not just *getting through* it—slowing down a little isn't necessarily a bad thing! In fact, slowing down and reading out loud has some terrific benefits.

You will focus more easily.

I have found nothing—other than prayer—that keeps my mind from wandering more effectively than reading out loud. Nothing. When I read silently, it is so easy to let my mind drift from one thought to the next.

How about you? Have you ever gotten a paragraph or two into your Bible reading only to discover you are thinking about something coming up later in your day? Have you ever been reading the Bible, turned the page, and had no idea why? *Well, my eyes were at the bottom. Where was I going to go—the margin?*

Reading out loud hasn't completely solved the problem, but it has helped immensely. Truth be told, there is nothing that will help you focus every time, all the time. That is as ridiculous as the running back who walks over to the coach and says, "Put me in, Coach. I have figured out a way to never get tackled." (Note: If you are a coach, you *can't* put that kid in. He has a concussion.)

Yes, my mind still wanders. In fact, sometimes it wanders two minutes into my reading. But since I started reading out loud, that is really rare. It has become so effective at helping me focus that the only time I *don't* read out loud is if I am in a place where I would be bothering someone. In a coffee shop. On a plane.

I once said that at a workshop only to have someone say, "You should go ahead and read out loud on the plane. Captive audience. Where are they going to go?" Nice. Maybe I will give it a try.

You will *hear* the Bible differently.

When you read the Bible, does it all sound the same in your head? More specifically, when you read Philippians and you read Galatians, do these two letters sound the same? If so—and please pardon my bluntness—you are reading incorrectly. Yes, they are both letters. Yes, they are both written by the apostle Paul. Yes, they are roughly the same length. Yes, they are both printed using the same font in your Bible. But they are massively different in how they sound.

Imagine you just received a letter. It is from a dear friend whom you love. You haven't seen this friend in a few years. The very first thing you read (out loud) is:

> Every time I think of you, I give thanks to my God. Whenever I pray, I make my requests for all of you with joy, for you have been my partners in spreading the Good News about Christ from the time you first heard it until now. And I am certain that God, who began the good work within you, will continue his work until it is finally finished on the day when Christ Jesus returns.
>
> So it is right that I should feel as I do about all of you, for you have a special place in my heart. You share with me the special favor of God, both in my imprisonment and in defending and confirming the truth of the Good News. God knows how much I love you and long for you with the tender compassion of Christ Jesus.
>
> Philippians 1:3–8 NLT

How do you feel? Loved? Cared for? Missed? Hugged?

Now, on a different day you receive another letter from the same friend. Out loud, you read these opening paragraphs:

> I am shocked that you are turning away so soon from God, who called you to himself through the loving mercy of Christ. You are following a different way that pretends to be the Good

News but is not the Good News at all. You are being fooled by those who deliberately twist the truth concerning Christ.

Let God's curse fall on anyone, including us or even an angel from heaven, who preaches a different kind of Good News than the one we preached to you. I say again what we have said before: If anyone preaches any other Good News than the one you welcomed, let that person be cursed.

Galatians 1:6–9 NLT

How do you feel now? Rebuked? A bit ashamed? Kicked in the backside?

The Bible is filled with so many different stories, characters, scenes, and emotions. Reading out loud brings all those voices to the surface. When I read silently, there is this little guy who jumps into my brain and reads my Bible for me. You might not know his name, but I suspect he has shown up in your brain as well. I call him Mr. Monotone.

Has Mr. Monotone ever read your Bible for you? *Blah, blah, blah*. How quickly we forget that we are reading the very words of God Almighty! The Author of Life has written you a letter. The Inventor of Words has breathed out the Living Word. And yet we allow Mr. Monotone to kill it.

You will remember more.

We remember some of what we see. We remember much more of what we see *and* hear. Even if what we are hearing is our own voice.

One frequently cited communications study compared what focus groups recalled if they were presented information only verbally, only visually, or both verbally and visually. The results were staggering. They found that after just seventy-two hours, participants retained only 10 percent of information presented verbally. Those who received the information visually retained 20 percent. Here's the kicker: Those who both heard and saw the information retained 65 percent of the information! It was the *combination* of seeing and hearing that made the difference.*

The same is true with the Bible. We will certainly retain some of what we read silently. But if you can more than triple your retention simply by reading out loud, why wouldn't you do it? It is frustrating to put time into reading something and not remembering it. Remembering what we read is a huge part of enjoying the Bible. And the best way to do that is to read out loud.

*Reported by Harold Weiss and J. B. McGrath, *Technically Speaking* (New York: McGraw-Hill, 1963), 77–78.

Study Guide for Tip 6

Raise Your Voice

Frequently, we are too quiet and serious when we read the Bible. Of course there are serious issues discussed. Certainly there are times when quiet reflection—or even complete silence—is the perfect response.

But not always. Not every time.

We miss so much of the story if we never read out loud—if we never allow ourselves to hear God speak, hear the people's voices, hear the sounds of battle, or singing, or shouting, or wailing. If the living Word of God is truly going to live, sometimes we need to let it live—out loud.

——— For the Group ———————————————————

1. Are you an "out loud" Bible reader? What has been your experience when you have read it out loud? What about when someone else reads it out loud (in church, Bible study, family devotions, etc.)?

2. Take a minute and read Philippians 1:3–8 and Galatians 1:6–9 again (preferably from your own Bible), out loud and with emotion. What is your initial reaction? What is Paul's tone? What would be your response if you were the original recipient of each letter?

3. Read the book of Jonah out loud. It'll take you about seven minutes. Read it with expression and feeling, like you were reading *Curious George* to a five-year-old. How did this familiar story sound to you? What stood out? What had you never noticed before? Try this with various sections of Genesis or one of the Gospels.

4. A study found that we remember 10 percent of what we hear, 20 percent of what we see, and 65 percent of what we hear and see. Does your experience line up with these findings? Try reading out loud for a week, and write down your experience of how much you remember (and how you feel about it). You can also read in the morning and then listen to the same passage (in your car or on your MP3 player or phone) later in the day.

—— Scripture to Soak In ————————————————

- Genesis 37–50 (It'll take about an hour, but it's an amazing story!)
- Jonah
- John 2
- Romans 10:16–18
- Hebrews 4:12–13

SHALL WE PRAY?

*Lord Jesus, the One who lives, the One who breathed life
into the Living Word, the One who is the Living Word,
Help me to hear Your Word today. Help me to see
the people in Scripture as real people, not characters in a
cosmic play. Help me to hear the various parts of Your
Word differently. I confess that there are many days when
I allow the monotone voice in my head to overshadow the
life in Your Word. May that not be true today. And may
my faith grow as I hear Your Word.*
Amen.

Tip 7

Read Alone

Most of the tips in this book are of the every-time-and-all-the-time variety. Tip 4 (Watch the Whole Movie) and Tip 5 (Learn From Your Shampoo Bottle) are done specifically when you are beginning a new study of a book or large section of the Bible.

This tip goes right along with those two. It is done at the start of your study. It helps you enjoy the Bible right from the get-go. It sets the stage for enjoying more detailed study later on. And it is something that most people tell me they rarely do (if ever).

Read *only* the Bible.

No devotional. No commentary. No questions. No videos. No lesson.

Yes, read alone.

Simply you, God, and His Word. That's it.

Now, before you fire off an email sharing how beneficial your last devotional was, all the ways a specific commentary has helped you, or what you have gleaned from a certain author's insights, hear me out. I love my study tools. The amount of research we have at the click of a mouse is phenomenal. I have no intention of ever giving up my Logos Bible Software. I read a lot of extra books and commentaries. *Just not at the beginning.*

Probably the best way to make my argument for reading alone is to look at what happens when we *don't* read alone. More specifically, what myths we end up believing when God's Word is always viewed through additional lenses.

Myth One: "A Bible commentary carries the same weight as Scripture."

Of course, we would never say this out loud. We would never say a commentary is actually God-breathed. But sometimes we unintentionally treat it that way. How can we not? When we read a commentary or devotional every time we read the Bible, our brains process them as equals.

Ironically, the most common culprit is a tool that is designed to do exactly the opposite. It is designed to help us know the Word and apply the Word. I have several of them myself. What is the culprit? Your study Bible.

Again, I love my study Bibles. I refer to them quite frequently. However, when I am kicking off a new study, I leave them on the shelf. I purposefully have another Bible that has almost no notes. Otherwise, I will be tempted to read every note. The temptation will win because I am a recovering "ping-pong reader."

Are you a ping-pong reader? Here is a simple test. When you are reading along in your Bible and come to a bold "a," do you feel an immediate and overwhelming obligation to "ping" down to the bottom of the page, read the note, and then "pong" (bounce) back up to the top? Then comes that bold "b." Ping . . . read the note. Pong . . . back up to the verse. Ping . . . pong. That's me. I am a ping-pong reader. It is virtually impossible for me not to bounce down to the notes. They are frequently so helpful. They shed so much light and provide clarity. The notes offer application and discussion questions. The maps and diagrams help me visualize what I am reading.

But they are not Scripture.

If we read them just as much as we read the biblical text—especially in the ping-pong style—how can we *not* give them the same amount of weight? I am reminded of something I heard a couple of decades ago. (Sorry, I can't remember who said it.)

A commentary is nothing more than another Christian's comments on the Bible.

Amen. The notes, books, devotionals, and commentaries are extremely helpful. They offer additional insight, explanation, and perspective we might never come up with on our own.

This is quite similar to the insight a friend might offer. If you are both reading the same book of the Bible, you will each see things the other missed. The conversation will benefit you both. But imagine if every time you got together you said, "I didn't read the Bible at all. What has God told you? What do I need to know? What encouragement do you have for me?"

Seems wrong, doesn't it? You would almost certainly learn some things. You might even enjoy their insights or marvel at how close they are to God. But you would be no closer to enjoying the Bible yourself, let alone falling in love with the Author!

Myth Two: "I can't understand the Bible unless someone explains it to me."

So many of us believe this myth. Do you? Answer honestly. Do you feel like the Bible is complicated? I spent a long time feeling overwhelmed by the Bible. Don't get me wrong. There is still plenty about the Bible I don't understand. After all, God put a lot in there!

That said, I no longer believe that the Bible is primarily difficult. In fact, I believe the opposite. The more I read it, the more I am convinced that a vast majority of what is written in the Bible can be understood by your average eleven-year-old. And yet, the myth lives on.

Let's put your God-given imagination to work. Rewind a few thousand years. You are a fly on the wall in the Throne Room, and Father, Son, and Spirit are having a conversation.

Father: "We should provide our children with a written relationship guide."

Son: "Fantastic idea! But I think we should make it as confusing as possible."

Holy Spirit: "Couldn't agree more. Oh . . . and it should probably be boring too."

What do you think? Absurd, right? This is the same Father who loved you and chose you before the creation of the world (Ephesians 1:4). This is the same Son who put on flesh, became the Living Word (John 1:1–18), allowed himself to be arrested, tortured, and killed, and then conquered death, hell, and the grave so you could hang out with Him forever. This is the same Holy Spirit who guides you (John 16:13) and intercedes with the Father on your behalf (Romans 8:26–27).

Would this Father, this Son, and this Holy Spirit really try to make understanding His Story something only a few theologians could grasp? A few teachers? A few pastors? While the rest were left to wallow in their confusion? Not a chance.

Debunk the myths.

You are almost done with this chapter. It is time for you to debunk these myths once and for all.

Go pour another cup of coffee. Grab a Bible. (Preferably one with very few notes.) Pick a book. And read. Just you and God. Ask Him to meet you there. Expect Him to meet you there. He will. After all, He has made a habit of doing exactly that for a very long time.

Study Guide for Tip 7

Read Alone

We are surrounded by so many voices. So many books. So many websites and blogs. So many preachers, teachers, and people who "know more" than we do.

And guess what?

God wants to hang out with you. He desires some highly personal, one-on-one time. With you. Just you.

He wants to speak to you. He wants to comfort you. He wants to restore you. He wants to teach you. He wants to correct you. He wants to heal you. He wants to laugh with you. He wants to uncover the mystery of His Word for you. He wants to read His Word to you and with you. (Yes, you.)

For the Group

1. Do you ever read *just* the Bible? If not, what are the books, resources, websites, or study tools you always read? Why?

2. *Myth One: "A Bible commentary carries the same weight as Scripture."* Are you a ping-pong reader? Force yourself to not be a ping-pong reader for a week. (This might require reading from a different Bible with no notes, or reading off-line if you're always tempted to go look it up on your favorite website.) Write down your experience of reading just the Word.

3. *Myth Two: "I can't understand the Bible unless someone explains it to me."* Do you believe this? I don't mean intellectually believe this. I mean experientially believe it. Is there a little voice that tells you that you're not smart enough, old enough, or well-read enough to understand the Bible? Talk with God about it. Confess the struggle. Then press on. Record what happens here. (And make sure you share it with the group.)

4. Get a few friends together and do a "pure" manuscript study. Go to www.biblegateway.com and copy/paste *just the text* from a book of the Bible into a Word document. Once you have the whole book in Word, remove all the chapter and verse numbers. Print it out. Biblegateway.com also includes the option to display passages without verse numbers, headings, and cross references (but chapter numbers are retained). Read only the text and see how much you come to understand—and enjoy—the natural breaks, the themes, and even the individual parts that stand out to you. Get together and discuss what you see with your group. I know many people who love manuscript studies so much that they rarely ever study the Bible any other way.

—— Scripture to Soak In ——

- Psalm 56:9
- Psalm 139
- Jeremiah 31:31–34
- Luke 12:1–7
- Ephesians 1:15–23

SHALL WE PRAY?

Abba Father, Jesus, Counselor,

I confess that many times it is easier to picture You as distant or removed, simply looking down on this world You created. I confess that sometimes I believe the lie that You can't speak to me. The lie that I can't understand Your Word. The lie that I can't know You. Help me see these for the lies that they are.

I need Your help to remember the truth. The truth that You are present with me as I read. The truth that You have chosen me and love me. The truth that You can—and will—reveal Yourself to me. The truth that You are here, that You are with me, and that You are for me.

Amen.

Tip 8

Don't Read Alone

Do I have you confused? I just suggested that you should first read longer sections of the Bible or a whole book alone—no devotionals, no commentaries, and so on. Now I am saying don't read alone. Which is it? Well, both, actually. It all has to do with timing. If we are talking about daily time in God's Word, "alone" is the answer. If we are talking about weekly, biweekly, or monthly, the answer expands to "alone *and* not alone."

When it comes to enjoying the Bible, few habits are more beneficial than having regular conversations with someone—or a small group of people—who is studying the same book of the Bible as you. There are at least four specific ways having a Bible buddy (yeah, cheesy, I know) will help you.

1. Your buddy will help you be more consistent.

Let's be honest. There is nothing quite like knowing that some-one will be checking up on you to improve your consistency. Yes, we should want to read the Bible. Yes, we should pursue our relationship with Christ because that's what we were made for. Yes, time with God in His Word should be at the top of our priority list. These are all true. But take a look at this:

> Let us hold tightly without wavering to the hope we affirm, for God can be trusted to keep his promise. Let us think of ways to motivate one another to acts of love and good works. And let us not neglect our meeting together, as some people do, but encourage one another, especially now that the day of his return is drawing near.
>
> Hebrews 10:23–25 NLT

Did you notice that three different times the author says "Let us." (That phrase shows up a whole bunch of times in Hebrews, by the way.) We were meant to be in this together. We need each other. God knows that we are easily distracted. God knows there are days when internal motivation is enough and days when, unfortunately, it is not.

We hate the feeling of committing to something and then having to look that person in the eyes and say, "No. I didn't get the reading done." Oooo . . . you hate that, don't you? Simply telling someone you will read—and scheduling a time to discuss it—will make you more consistent. Ideal or not, it just works.

2. Your buddy will make it more fun.

Remember attending summer camp or being in Girl Scouts or Boy Scouts? Wasn't there always a buddy system? The main reason for the buddy system was safety. But it was also more fun. Whether you were canoeing on the lake, hiking the trails, or practicing archery—it was far more fun with a buddy. Having a Bible buddy is also more fun. When someone gets excited, you get excited. When someone sees something as funny, you are more likely to see it as funny. When someone shares something that challenged them, you will find yourself wondering how you could apply that truth.

There is a concept I have written about in a couple of other books that applies here: *Whatever we talk about, we get more interested in.*

Think about anything you love. Music. Sports. Movies. Coffee. Ice cream. (These are some of my favorites.) Whatever the topic, how did you first get into it? Chances are pretty high that you knew someone who introduced you to a certain type of music, took you to a ballgame, or taught you how to make perfect foam for your cappuccino. You experienced it with someone. You talked about it. You spent time with someone who loved it, and you started to love it.

We love to talk, and we talk about what we love. Maybe you couldn't care less about sports. Maybe you enjoy knitting. If so, are there people you could get together with who could talk about yarn, patterns, and past projects all day long?

You can get that way with the Bible. You *will* get that way with the Bible. But not if you always—and only—read alone. You need someone to talk with about what you read. You need a buddy.

3. Your buddy will see things you missed.

You can't catch everything. You won't catch everything. You weren't meant to catch everything. We need each other. This is a good thing.

Solomon wasn't kidding when he wrote:

As iron sharpens iron, so a friend sharpens a friend.

Proverbs 27:17 NLT

Left alone, the sharpest knife will grow dull. It needs to be sharpened. So do you. So do I. We need each other if we are going to be as sharp as we can possibly be. A knife can't sharpen itself. Neither can you.

It never ceases to amaze me how different people will see so many different details, truths, or applications in the same passage. I can pour over a passage time and again, feeling like I have gleaned everything there is to glean. Inevitably, when I get together with a buddy, he will bring up something that I completely missed.

The same thing happens in our small group each week. We all bring something different to the conversation. As we each share what God has revealed to us, we are all encouraged, challenged, and learn. As we do, each of us continually grows in our love for God and His Word.

Whether you meet one-on-one with a buddy, gather with a few other men or women, or get a handful of couples together every other week, you need to read with other people. Until you do, you will be tasting only a small sliver of a really big pie. And come on, who doesn't like more pie?

4. Your buddy will help you clarify your own thinking.

Thoughts that stay in your head remain cloudy. As they move through your mind and out your mouth, they will simply sound different. You will realize that what you thought to be true was slightly off. Or the conviction of your mind might become even stronger as you talk about it. Either way, there is great value in talking with another person (or group of people) about what God has been saying to you.

This is very similar to what happens when we journal. I have frequently heard a quote from Dawson Trotman, founder of The Navigators, that I completely agree with:

> "Thoughts disentangle themselves passing over the lips or through pencil tips."

There is something that happens when we talk things out that is freeing and clarifying. It happens when we journal. It happens even more fully when we add discussion to the mix.

Ask a friend if she wants to meet for coffee before work each Tuesday. Find a few friends who will grab lunch with you on Thursdays. See if four other couples would set aside every other Sunday evening for dinner and discussion.

Now pick a book of the Bible and have each person read it on their own. When you get together, unpack it. For a couple of weeks, you might chat about the overarching big themes each person noticed. Then start to narrow it down. Discuss a chapter, a story, or even a single verse. Watch what happens.

My prediction? You will find yourself enjoying the Bible more and looking forward to the next time your group is getting together.

Study Guide for Tip 8

Don't Read Alone

I know I pushed this tip really hard. I did it because it is super important—almost "nonnegotiable" type of important. Let me put it this way:

> I have never met anyone who has participated
> in a small-group discussion and said it
> wasn't both beneficial and enjoyable.

There is a chance you are walking through these study questions alone. You think you can do it on your own. You think you don't need a partner in this. After all, you've made it this far. You are on Tip 8!

But remember this: The goal is not to get through the Bible, this book, or these study questions. The goal is to enjoy the Bible—to enjoy building an ever-deepening relationship with Jesus.

To do that, you need a partner.

For the Group

1. If you are reluctant to get a Bible buddy (or small group of buddies), why is that? Don't have time? Don't need to talk about it? Too private? Whatever the reason, clearly identify it here.

2. Is consistency a struggle for you? What *are* you consistent at? Is it something you do alone? Is it beneficial? Is it something that brings you joy?

3. Revisit this quote:

   "Whatever we talk about, we get more interested in."

   Where have you seen this to be true in your own life? What are your hobbies? How do you spend your time? Can you trace it back to someone who introduced you to it or talked with you about it?

4. Have you ever been a part of a small-group discussion and been blown away by what other people saw in a section of the Bible that you totally missed? (Or shared something someone else didn't see?) Was it beneficial or encouraging? Is there any reason you wouldn't want to put yourself in a situation where that could happen more frequently?

5. Do you consider yourself a verbal processor? Do you like to journal? What is your reaction to the following quote?

"Thoughts disentangle themselves passing over the lips or through pencil tips."

Dawson Trotman, founder of The Navigators

Scripture to Soak In

- Proverbs 27:17
- Ecclesiastes 4:9–12
- Colossians 1:9–14
- 1 Thessalonians 5:11
- Hebrews 10:24–25

SHALL WE PRAY?

Father, Son, and Spirit,

In Your very essence, You exemplify Your design and desire for community. You live in community with Yourself and with us—Your children. Although I can't fully fathom it, I know it is true.

When I am tempted to walk this journey alone, remind me that I need other brothers and sisters in Christ. I need them to encourage me. I need them to correct me. I need them to walk beside me. I need them to comfort me. I need them to teach me. I need them to sharpen me. I need them.

Amen.

Tip 9

Go on a 60-Day Adventure

What would you say if I told you that sixty days from now you could understand and love a book of the Bible more than any you have studied before? Now, what if I told you that you would actually have huge chunks of it down word-for-word without even trying? That would be pretty cool, right?

Well, you can. (Yes, you.)

In my first book—*Falling in Love With God's Word: Discovering What God Always Intended Bible Study to Be*—I lay out my entire approach for how I study the Bible. I am not going to try to explain the whole process here, but I do want to give you the basics.

As you have gathered by now, when we approach the Bible the same way our brains naturally and easily learn anything else (from the general to the specific), we enjoy it more and remember it better. In that first book, I put the process into the analogy of building a house. Foundation first. Then Framing. Finally, Finish Work. All are vitally important. So is the *order* in which we do them.

Before laying out the day-by-day plan, here is the ultra-nutshell version of each phase:

Foundation

This is where you get the big picture. This is where Tip 4, Tip 5, and Tip 7 come in. Read a whole book of the Bible. Read it again. Read alone. This is where you get a feel for the main topics, tone, and thought process of the book.

During the Foundation phase is also where you do some background studies on the author, the audience, and the atmosphere. There are lots of tools—online and in print—to help you with this. For more information, you can check out www .keithferrin.com/resources.

Framing

The Framing phase is essentially where you build a bridge between the general study of Foundation and the paragraph-by-paragraph, detailed study found in Finish Work. First, break down the book into major sections. Possibly put it into an outline. I know, the word *outline* might make you cringe with bad memories from high school, but it is very efficient.

Break it down one step further to see where each paragraph or two fits into the broader outline. This isn't the time to study each paragraph. You are just putting it into smaller pieces. Think of the first step as the acts of a play and the second as jotting down the scenes that make up the acts.

Finish Work

Once you have laid a Foundation and done the very quick but very necessary Framing, you are ready for Finish Work. This is when you look for specific life application. Finish Work is the time for meditating on a single paragraph or verse. Study a word or phrase that has shown up several times in that book. Again, there are lots of resources out there to help you with this. During Finish Work is when I am extremely grateful for my study Bible, numerous Bible websites, and my Logos Bible Software.

"What book should I use for the 60-Day Adventure?"

I almost always recommend starting with either Philippians or 2 Timothy. The main reason is quite simple: *They are both short.* Anytime you are trying something new, short is good. Philippians takes about fifteen to twenty minutes to read. Second Timothy is even shorter. You can easily read either book in a single sitting, whether you have been in the habit of Bible reading or you are just starting out.

There is one more reason I recommend these two books in particular. Each contains a lot of what I refer to as the "Christian cliché" verses. Not cliché as in lame or silly. *Cliché* as in verses we hear all the time. Have you ever heard any of these?

- "I thank my God every time I remember you." (Philippians)
- "For God has not given us a spirit of fear and timidity, but of power, love, and self-discipline." (2 Timothy NLT)
- "For to me, to live is Christ and to die is gain." (Philippians)

- "And the things you have heard me say in the presence of many witnesses entrust to reliable people who will also be qualified to teach others." (2 Timothy)
- "And the peace of God, which transcends all understanding, will guard your hearts and your minds in Christ Jesus." (Philippians)
- "All Scripture is God-breathed. . . ." (2 Timothy)
- "Rejoice in the Lord always. I will say it again: Rejoice!" (Philippians)
- "I have fought the good fight, I have finished the race, I have kept the faith." (2 Timothy)
- "I can do everything through Christ, who gives me strength." (Philippians NLT)

Both books contain a lot more than what's listed here. And yet, if I asked you what Philippians is about or to summarize 2 Timothy in a sentence or two, could you do it? When you dive into either of these letters for a couple of months, it fills in the gaps. It helps you see these familiar verses in a new light. It provides context. People tell me all the time how much more they understand—and enjoy—the books after soaking in the big picture.

A 60-Day Adventure in Philippians

Foundation

Day

1   Read Philippians. (Out loud. Remember Tip 6!)

2   Read Philippians.

3   Read Philippians.

4   Read Philippians as if you were Paul sitting in prison.

Day

5   Read Philippians. Do a background study on the author (Paul). Information can be found in your study Bible, or visit www.keithferrin.com/resources.

6   Read Philippians using a different Bible translation.

7   Read Philippians.

8   Read Philippians as if you were a member of the Philippian church receiving this letter for the first time.

9   Read Philippians. Do a background study on the audience (church in Philippi).

10   Read Philippians. Write a one-paragraph summary of Philippians. (Don't overthink this.)

11   Read Philippians. Make a list of the main themes found in Philippians.

12   Read Philippians.

13   Read Philippians. Do a background study on the atmosphere. (What was going on at the time? Again, your study Bible will help you, or visit www.keith ferrin.com/resources.)

14   Read Philippians in a third translation (other than your normal Bible and what you read on Day 6).

15   Read Philippians. Review the summary you wrote on Day 10. See if you can narrow it down to two or three sentences.

16   Read Philippians. Form the themes you identified on Day 11 into a very general outline.

17   Read Philippians.

18   Read Philippians.

19   Read Philippians.

Day

20 Read Philippians. Pare down what you wrote on Days 10 and 15 into one or two sentences.

21 Read Philippians. Review the outline you wrote on Day 16. Can it be simplified or clarified?

22 Read Philippians in a fourth translation. (Maybe try one of the paraphrases like *The Message* or *The Voice Bible*.)

23 Read Philippians.

24 Read Philippians.

25 Read Philippians. Take what you wrote on Day 20 and get it down to a single concise sentence. (This forms a summary or purpose statement for the book.)

26 Read Philippians. Finalize the outline you wrote on Day 21.

Framing

Day

27 Read Philippians 1. Take the outline you finalized on Day 21. Break it down one or two more levels based on each paragraph in chapter 1.

28 Read Philippians 2. Take the outline you finalized on Day 21. Break it down one or two more levels based on each paragraph in chapter 2.

29 Read Philippians 3. Take the outline you finalized on Day 21. Break it down one or two more levels based on each paragraph in chapter 3.

Day

30   Read Philippians 4. Take the outline you finalized on
      Day 21. Break it down one or two more levels based
      on each paragraph in chapter 4.

Finish Work

During the Finish Work phase, it is time to focus on a few
verses or even a single word. You could read it prayerfully, engaging with God about what you read. You might try journaling,
writing a song, or drawing a picture. If you teach the Bible, you
will find it helpful to add anything you discover through prayer
or study to a more detailed version of your outline.

Word studies can be done online (see www.keithferrin.com/
resources), using purchased software, or by obtaining a good
Bible dictionary or word study book. Feel free to shoot me a
note if you need help getting pointed in the right direction.
There is also a whole chapter devoted to this in my first book,
Falling in Love With God's Word.

In any event, a major focus of Finish Work is not just understanding the verses for the day, but also *applying* what God
shows you. Life application is how God uses His Word to transform us to be more like Jesus. After all, head knowledge without
application will never lead to loving God and His Word!

Day

31   Focus on Philippians 1:1–2. Do a word study on
      "servant/bondservant/slave."*

32   Focus on 1:3–6. Do a word study on "joy."

*Many Greek and Hebrew words can be translated into different English words
and phrases. I have accounted for the word variances of the six most common
translations: NIV, KJV, NKJV, ESV, NASB, and NLT. If you use a translation
other than one of these, your wording might be slightly different. As a point of
reference, the first word shown in this word study is always from the NIV.

Day

33   Focus on 1:7–8.

34   Focus on 1:9–11. Do a word study on "pure/sincere."

35   Focus on 1:12–14.

36   Focus on 1:15–18a (the first part of the verse).

37   Do a word study on "selfish ambition/contention."

38   Focus on 1:18b (the second part of the verse)–26.

39   Do a word study on "hope."

40   Read Philippians.

41   Focus on 1:27–30.

42   Focus on 2:1–4.

43   Do a word study on "fellowship/participation."

44   Focus on 2:5–11.

45   Do a word study on "nature/form." Notice how different Greek words are translated the same in verses 6 and 7.

46   Focus on 2:12–13.

47   Focus on 2:14–18.

48   Focus on 2:19–24.

49   Focus on 2:25–30. Do a word study on "honor/reputation/high regard/esteem."

50   Read Philippians.

51   Focus on 3:1–6.

52   Focus on 3:7–11.

53   Do a word study on "righteousness."

54   Focus on 3:12–16.

55   Focus on 3:17–4:1.

56   Focus on 4:2–9.

57   Do a word study on "anxious/careful/worry."

Day

58 Focus on 4:10–13. Do a word study on "content."

59 Focus on 4:14–23.

60 Read Philippians.

A 60-Day Adventure in 2 Timothy

Foundation

Day

1 Read 2 Timothy. (Out loud. Remember Tip 6!)

2 Read 2 Timothy.

3 Read 2 Timothy.

4 Read 2 Timothy as if you were Paul sitting on death row, knowing you won't make it through the winter.

5 Read 2 Timothy. Do a background study on the author (Paul). Information can be found in your study Bible, or visit www.keithferrin.com/resources.

6 Read 2 Timothy in a different translation.

7 Read 2 Timothy.

8 Read 2 Timothy as if you were Timothy. Your good friend and mentor, Paul, is writing from death row with some final words and a desperate plea to come visit him soon.

9 Read 2 Timothy. Do a background study on the audience (Timothy).

10 Read 2 Timothy. Write a one-paragraph summary of 2 Timothy. (Don't overthink this.)

11 Read 2 Timothy. Make a list of the main themes found in 2 Timothy.

Day

12   Read 2 Timothy.

13   Read 2 Timothy. Do a background study on the at-mosphere. (What was going on at the time? Again, your study Bible will help you or visit www.keith ferrin.com/resources.)

14   Read 2 Timothy in a third translation (other than your normal Bible and what you read on Day 6).

15   Read 2 Timothy. Review the summary you wrote on Day 10. See if you can narrow it down to two or three sentences.

16   Read 2 Timothy. Form the themes you identified on Day 11 into a very general outline.

17   Read 2 Timothy.

18   Read 2 Timothy.

19   Read 2 Timothy.

20   Read 2 Timothy. Pare down what you wrote on Days 10 and 15 into one or two sentences.

21   Read 2 Timothy. Review the outline you wrote on Day 16. Can it be simplified or clarified?

22   Read 2 Timothy in a fourth translation. (Maybe try one of the paraphrases like *The Message* or *The Voice Bible*.)

23   Read 2 Timothy.

24   Read 2 Timothy.

25   Read 2 Timothy. Take what you wrote on Day 20 and get it down to a single concise sentence. (This forms a summary or purpose statement for the book.)

26   Read 2 Timothy. Finalize the outline you wrote on Day 21.

Framing

Day

27 Read 2 Timothy 1. Take the outline you finalized on Day 21. Break it down one or two more levels based on each paragraph in chapter 1.

28 Read 2 Timothy 2. Take the outline you finalized on Day 21. Break it down one or two more levels based on each paragraph in chapter 2.

29 Read 2 Timothy 3. Take the outline you finalized on Day 21. Break it down one or two more levels based on each paragraph in chapter 3.

30 Read 2 Timothy 4. Take the outline you finalized on Day 21. Break it down one or two more levels based on each paragraph in chapter 4.

Finish Work

During the Finish Work phase, it is time to focus on a few verses or even a single word. You could read it prayerfully, engaging with God about what you read. You might try journaling, writing a song, or drawing a picture. If you teach the Bible, you will find it helpful to add anything you discover through prayer or study to a more-detailed version of your outline.

Word studies can be done online, using purchased software, or by obtaining a good Bible dictionary or word study book. Feel free to shoot me a note if you need help getting pointed in the right direction.

In any event, a major focus of Finish Work is not just understanding the verses for the day, but also *applying* what God shows you. Life application is how God uses His Word to transform us to be more like Jesus. After all, head knowledge without application will never lead to loving God and His Word!

Day

31   Focus on 2 Timothy 1:1–5.

32   Do a word study on "apostle."*

33   Focus on 1:6–7.

34   Focus on 1:8–12.

35   Focus on 1:13–14.

36   Do a word study on "guard/keep."

37   Focus on 1:15–18.

38   Focus on 2:1–7.

39   Focus on 2:8–13. Do a word study on "endure/ suffer."

40   Read 2 Timothy.

41   Focus on 2:14–19.

42   Do a word study on "correctly handles/rightly dividing/rightly handling/correctly explains."

43   Focus on 2:20–21.

44   Do a word study on "made holy/sanctified/set apart as holy/clean."

45   Focus on 2:22–26.

46   Focus on 3:1–5.

47   Do a word study (or several!) on any of the words in 3:1–5.

48   Focus on 3:6–9.

---

*Many Greek and Hebrew words can be translated into different English words and phrases. I have accounted for the word variances of the six most common translations: NIV, KJV, NKJV, ESV, NASB, and NLT. If you use a translation other than one of these, your wording might be slightly different. As a point of reference, the first word shown in this word study is always from the NIV.

Day

49   Focus on 3:10–13.

50   Read 2 Timothy.

51   Focus on 3:14–17.

52   Do a word study on "God-breathed/inspired by God/
     given by inspiration/breathed out by God."

53   Focus on 4:1–2.

54   Focus on 4:3–5.

55   Focus on 4:6–8.

56   Focus on 4:9–13.

57   Focus on 4:14–15.

58   Focus on 4:16–18.

59   Focus on 4:19–22.

60   Read 2 Timothy.

Study Guide for Tip 9

Go on a 60-Day Adventure

Two months. Sixty days. That's all that I am asking for (until the next chapter).

What if I told you that sixty days from now, you could know and love a book of the Bible more than you ever have before? What if I told you that you could talk through all the major themes and sections of an entire book? What if I told you that two months from now, you could have huge chunks of that book—even *most* of the book—internalized word for word?

You can. Give me sixty days. That's all I'm asking.

For the Group

Each of the next few pages can be used to jot down notes at various points in the 60-Day Adventure. Sometimes you will be revisiting an element (e.g., the book's purpose statement), and it is helpful to see them all in the same place. If you are not going to use these pages, I recommend creating a Word document and keeping all of your notes, revisions, word studies, etc., in one place.

Finally, the 60-Day Adventure takes a more serious commitment of daily time (about twenty to thirty minutes each day). If your buddy or group is committed to staying on the same schedule, you will find tremendous benefit in doing a 60-Day Adventure together. However, I recognize that some groups want to study a book of the Bible, but members (for a whole host of reasons) might not be able to commit to an "every day" plan. An adapted plan for groups (using the book of Ephesians) is found in appendix A.

SHALL WE PRAY?

Living Word,
   As I embark on this journey, guide me into Your truth and Your presence. When the distractions and excuses come, show me what they truly are—an attempt of the enemy to keep me from soaking in Your Word and being transformed by Your Spirit.
   Help me remember that even this deep study is about my relationship with You. Help me remember that You are present as I read, study, and internalize Your Word. Help me remember that Your Word is the sword of the Spirit. Help me remember that while the battle before me is big, Your sword is much bigger and much more powerful. Thank You for what You will do in and through me.
   Amen.

Use this page to write down thoughts, questions, themes, and application as you do the first couple of weeks of reading through Philippians or 2 Timothy each day.

Background Study—Author

What can you learn about Paul from the text itself? You might want to consult your study Bible, a Bible dictionary, or an online study resource.

Background Study—Audience

What can you learn about the audience from the text itself? Was it written to one person or a group of people? Were they people Paul knew well or had just heard about? You might want to consult your study Bible, a Bible dictionary, or an online study resource.

Background Study—Atmosphere

What can you learn about the region that Paul—and the audience—lived in? What about the time period? What else was going on at the time? Was it a time of peace or persecution? You might want to consult your study Bible, a Bible encyclopedia, or an online study resource.

Summary (Purpose Statement)

I call the one-sentence summary of a book (finalized on Day 25) a purpose statement. It is not very hard to get to this purpose statement if you take it one small step at a time. The first step is to *not even start* until Day 10. Otherwise, it will be a very "heady" exercise. However, once you have read the book ten times, you will know it quite well. At that time, writing a summary will be a piece of cake.

Day 10: Write a one-paragraph summary of Philippians or 2 Timothy. (Don't overthink this.)

Day 15: Narrow your summary down to two or three sentences.

Day 20: Narrow your summary down to one or two sentences.

Day 25: Take what you wrote on Day 20 and get it down to a single concise sentence.

Word Studies

If you would like more in-depth instruction on how to do a word study, there is a whole chapter devoted to the process in my book *Falling in Love With God's Word*. You can also go to www.keithferrin.com and search for "word study." Use this page to jot down what you learn about the important words and phrases in Philippians and 2 Timothy.

Life Application

Years ago, I was inspired and deeply convicted when I read these words by Bob Shirock, senior pastor of Oak Pointe Church in Novi, Michigan:

> "You have not truly mastered any
> part of the Bible until that part of
> the Bible has mastered you."

This is where you jot down the conversations you have with God. Answer some of these questions (and any others you come up with):

- What is God telling you?
- Where is He leading you?
- What is He asking you to apply?
- Where is He correcting your thinking? Your behavior? Your attitude?
- What is God showing you about who He is?
- What is one step you will take today to be more like Jesus?

Just so you know, I hope you end up needing a lot more than one page!

Tip 10

Take Two 4-Month Challenges

B y now, you have probably noticed that I am a pretty big fan of the big picture. These two challenges will help you get the big picture. Two big pictures actually. Let's look at the first . . .

Challenge One: The Bible Read Thru

Until a few years ago, I didn't realize how helpful—and enjoyable—it would be to get the really, really big picture. Not until a woman who had taken my Falling in Love With God's Word workshop sent me an email with a link to an article by Ron Frost.

Ron is a pastoral consultant for Barnabas International and was a professor at Multnomah University for twenty years. The article tells of when he was a young man, and of a retired missionary who inspired him to simply read the Bible—two to three times every year! Ron took the challenge and has been doing exactly that for the last several decades. I was intrigued, to say the least.

Soon after reading the article, I reached out to Ron, and he agreed to have lunch with me. We sat at a small, waterfront restaurant in Seattle and chatted about our mutual love for the Living Word. I walked away knowing that I needed to do what Ron calls a Bible Read Thru.

I knew I had to do it. I knew it would be valuable. I just didn't want to. It seemed like too much time. I ignored the Voice for a couple of months. Then came New Year's, and along with it . . . resolutions. "Okay, God. I'll do it."

Heeding Ron's advice, I didn't try it alone. (Remember Tip 8?) I invited the men at my church's January men's breakfast to join me. Five other guys took the challenge. To a person, all six of us found it extremely enjoyable and valuable.

We were also blown away at how much easier it was than any of us expected. In fact, one of the guys finished in seventy-three days! *And he had never read the Bible before.* In fact, he didn't even own a Bible. The week before we started, he had to grab one of the paperback Bibles we hand out at church.

That first Bible Read Thru was started in January 2010. I have now done it every year since (and have no plans to stop anytime soon). It is my January-through-April ritual.

There are only three simple parameters:

1. Read the whole Bible in four months.

You can read Genesis to Revelation straight through. You can read using a chronological Bible. (One chronological plan is provided in appendix B.) You can read an Old Testament book, New Testament, then back to the Old Testament. However you want. Just read it. The whole thing.

If you are thinking this is an oh-my-goodness-I-could-never-do-that commitment, allow me to put it in perspective. The average audio Bible is a little over seventy hours. That even includes the sound effects for animals, musicians, and storms.

Multiply by sixty minutes and divide that by 122 (the number of days in a four-month stretch), and your daily commitment is about thirty-five minutes. Is it a step up from what you are doing now? Possibly. Is it an insurmountable challenge? Hardly. I highly encourage you to simply set aside forty-five to sixty minutes a day. That way, even allowing for the pauses to underline or jot down a quick note, you will always be ahead. There will be days when you can squeeze in only ten minutes because you are swamped with work, school, or your kid's baseball tournament. There will be days when you've got the flu and can't read at all. If you build in a habit of reading a little extra, those days won't set you back.

Whatever you do, don't break it down into how much you have to "get through" each day. Your mindset will be all wrong. It will very quickly become a chore. And when you miss a day, you will spend days or weeks playing catch-up. No fun. Even if you are following a chronological reading plan, use the breakdown as a guide for what passages you need to be reading, not the specific amount per day you have to get through.

2. Read with a pen in your hand.

If you are an "underliner," underline. If not, take notes in a journal. You can also use a virtual notepad like OneNote or Evernote. Find some way to keep track of the conversations you have with God as you read.

Whatever method you choose, it is important to remember that you are not outlining or writing down details. This is a Bible *Read Thru*. It is not a Bible *study*. Simply jot down anything that stands out, challenges you, or even confuses you. Stay in the big story. Who knows? The notes you jot down during this four-month stretch might just be the guide for the deeper study you do the rest of the year.

3. Talk about it.

If you want to get the most out of your Bible Read Thru, this third parameter is not optional. You will be tempted to make it optional. It will seem easier to keep it between you and God. You will convince yourself that you don't need the accountability to stick with it.

First off, accountability is a good thing, and you probably do need it. That said, accountability isn't the main reason the third parameter is in here. Remember: This book is about enjoying the Bible. Talking about it will help you enjoy it. That's why I devoted a whole chapter to having a Bible buddy.

Most of the time, I have gotten together with a group of three to six men. Last year, there were a couple of women who joined us. There was certainly value found in each scenario. I have no hard-and-fast guidance here.

However, I do recommend having a minimum of three people (and preferably four to six). That way, when someone is traveling, sick, or accidentally oversleeps, you don't end up skipping a week.

I have heard of people doing this part with their weekly small group, after school, or even with some coworkers over the lunch break. The Bible Read Thru groups I have assembled have always met at a coffee shop (my home away from home) early in the morning on a weekday.

When you get together, keep it very simple. First off, decide how much time you are going to spend just chatting. If you set aside ten minutes to catch up on family, work, or the weekend's ballgame, then you will stick to it. If you don't set a time, you will get thirty minutes in and someone will say, "Oh, look at the time. I guess we better hustle through this." Not the approach you are looking for.

Have each person share one of the things they wrote down or underlined. Read the passage if it's not too long. Focus on the

Word and the conversations you each had with God throughout the week. Resist the urge to answer every question or turn it into a discussion about what a passage means or what each of you thinks about what someone else shared. Keep in mind that you will have each read about fifty to eighty chapters of the Bible since you last met. If you have an in-depth conversation about every verse someone underlined, you will need to meet daily, not weekly!

Read the Bible in four months.

Read with a pen in your hand.

Talk about it.

That's it.

Take the challenge. Four months from now, your love for the Word, understanding of the Word, and appreciation of the Word will all be greatly increased.

Challenge Two: The New Disciple Challenge

I call this one the New Disciple Challenge, not because it is only for new Christ-followers, but because it is definitely where I recommend a new disciple to start. If you have only recently begun hanging out with Jesus, then you need to, well, hang out with Jesus.

Note: If you have been walking with Christ a long time, you might want to begin with a Bible Read Thru or one of the 60-Day Adventures from the last chapter. That said, I highly recommend taking this second challenge every so often just to keep your heart and mind focused on the person, work, teaching, and mission of Jesus.

The parameters for the New Disciple Challenge are even simpler than the last one:

1. *Focus on only five books.*

During these four months, you will read only Matthew, Mark, Luke, John, and Acts. Here is a quick overview of each:

- **Matthew**—Matthew (also known as Levi) was a tax collector who became one of Jesus' twelve disciples and traveled with Jesus during the approximately three years of His earthly ministry. He focuses pretty heavily on Jesus as the Messiah/King and how Jesus fulfills Old Testament prophecies (facts and predictions about future events).

- **Mark**—Mark (also known as John Mark) was not one of the twelve disciples. He traveled with the apostle Paul on his first missionary journey. He focuses on Jesus' humble servant attitude: what He did, what He taught, and how He lived.

- **Luke**—Luke was a doctor, as well as a close friend and traveling companion of the apostle Paul. He is the only known Gentile (non-Jewish) author in the New Testament. Luke is the "detail guy." He paints a clear picture of Jesus as the perfect Son of Man.

- **John**—John was one of the twelve disciples (so was his older brother James) and refers to himself as "the disciple Jesus loved." He is out to show his readers that Jesus is not only fully human, but He is fully God as well. As we come to know Jesus' humanity and divinity, we also see that real, abundant, eternal life can come only through Him.

- **Acts**—Luke is also the author of Acts. In the book of Acts, Luke gives an account of the formation, growth, success, and struggles of the early church. The first third of the book focuses primarily on the work and teaching of Peter (one of the twelve disciples). The latter two-thirds focuses on the conversion of the apostle Paul (previously a Christian hater and killer) and his three missionary journeys.

2. Read each book for two weeks.

There isn't a set number of times you need to read each book. Determine how much time you will set aside each day for reading. Obviously, if you read for forty-five minutes each day, you will read each book more times than if you read only for twenty. That said, even reading twenty minutes each day will have you walking through each book at least twice in a two-week period.

Some of you might be concerned about my math skills. Yes, this is a four-month challenge. Yes, you will read only five books. Yes, you will read each for two weeks. However, you will read Acts *after each Gospel*. Here's how it goes: Read Matthew for two weeks. Then read Acts for two weeks. Then Mark for two weeks. Back to Acts for two weeks. Then Luke. Then Acts. Then John. Finish with two weeks in Acts.

By the end of the four months, you will have read four different accounts of the life of Jesus and the history of the early church several times. This overview will provide an extremely solid foundation, whether your next study takes you back into the Old Testament or into a 60-Day Adventure into one of the letters of the New Testament.

3. Talk about it.

Yes, the Buddy Rule still applies. You will get far more out of it if you are reading with someone. It is vital—especially for new Christians—to develop a habit of meeting with others to discuss, question, wrestle with, and process God's Word.

If you skipped the last section about the Bible Read Thru—and you want to find out more about the benefits of this third parameter—hop back about a thousand words. It's all there waiting for you.

Study Guide for Tip 10

Take Two 4-Month Challenges

What I am about to say comes dangerously close to the edge of "too cheesy to put in print." I am going to say it anyhow.

I am excited for you! (I warned you.)

But I am. I am truly excited. If you are reading this sentence, then it is highly likely that you are seriously considering one (or both) of these 4-Month Challenges. I know the impact these next four months will have. I know how they will increase your love for the Word. I know how much more you will enjoy reading your Bible when you are done. I know how much more of the Bible you will know and understand. I know how these next four months will enhance every other Bible study you do moving forward. I know the foundation they will provide. I know that your heart and mind will soon echo this email I recently received. It is from someone on the other side of the world (literally) who took my challenge and is about halfway through her very first Bible Read Thru:

"The Lord has gradually begun to make it
easier for me to interact with His Word. I
am working on finishing the Bible by April,

and I have never been more excited. I
have been a Christian for years, and God's
Word has never been more alive!"

Can you see why I'm excited?

Challenge One: Bible Read Thru

Remember, this is far better if you keep it simple. Here are the
three parameters outlined in this chapter:

1. Read the whole Bible in four months.

There are lots of ways to do this. You can read straight
through, alternate between books of the Old Testament and
the New Testament, or even read some of the poetry books (like
Psalms and Proverbs) at a different time of the day.

By far, the two most common are reading straight through
from Genesis to Revelation or reading the Bible chronologically. (Note: Appendix B is a chronological reading plan you
can refer to.) In either case, it is really important to simply
set aside an amount of time you will read, as opposed to an
amount of content you will get through each day. Let's revisit
what I wrote in the chapter:

Whatever you do, don't break it down into
how much you have to "get through" each
day. Your mindset will be all wrong. It will
very quickly become a chore. And when you
miss a day, you will spend days or weeks

playing catch-up. No fun. Even if you are following a chronological reading plan, use the breakdown as a guide for what passages you need to be reading, not the specific amount per day you have to get through.

2. Read with a pen in your hand.

You've got to write things down if you want to remember them when it's time for discussion or application. That said, keep in mind that the purpose of these four months is to stay general, not to record a question or application for every verse. This is first and foremost about engaging with the story.

3. Talk about it.

By now, you're sick of hearing me say it. And yet, here I go again: If your goal is to enjoy the Bible more—and be more consistent—then you need a buddy (or a few buddies). You need to talk about it. You have to get together with people who are doing the Bible Read Thru with you. Together is better. Period.

Challenge Two: The New Disciple Challenge

If you are new to this Jesus-journey (or if you could simply use a refresher), this is the place to start. This will give you a terrific overview of the life of Jesus and the history of the early church. It will provide a foundation for when you dive into another book of the Bible—Old Testament or New Testament.

I won't rewrite the whole chapter here, but here again are the parameters:

1. Focus on only five books.

Matthew, Mark, Luke, and John are four accounts of the life of Jesus. They were written by people who were very different. The book of Acts was also written by Luke and provides an overview of the early church. It begins with the resurrected Jesus ascending into heaven and walks right on through the teachings of Peter and the missionary journeys of the apostle Paul. You'll read quite a bit about Luke and Mark in the book of Acts.

2. Read each book for two weeks.

There is no set number of times you need to read through each book. Set aside an amount of time you can read, and just read one book for two weeks. First, Matthew for two weeks. Then Acts for two weeks. Mark for two. Acts for two more. Luke for two weeks. Acts for another two. John for two weeks. Finally, finish with two more weeks of reading Acts.

3. Talk about it.

Scan back about three hundred words. The same thing still applies. Read. Get together. Talk about it.

SHALL WE PRAY?

Gracious Father, Resurrected Jesus, Guiding Spirit,
As I journey through the next four months, guide me into Your truth and Your presence. When the distractions and excuses come, show me what they truly are—an attempt of the enemy to keep me from soaking in Your Word and being transformed by Your Spirit.

I need the foundation these next four months will provide. I need to know Your story so I can better understand my own. I need to embrace Your story so I can live more fully in my own. I need to see Your presence in Your story so I can more quickly and easily recognize and respond to Your presence in my own.

As I read, remind me that this isn't just Your story with a completed beginning and ending. Your story is still unfolding—for You are the same yesterday, today, and forever. I recognize that my story is not my own. My story is enveloped completely in Your story. My story will best be lived and best be told when I let You live it in and through me. I am Yours. Remind me of that truth as I read.

Amen.

How These 10 Tips
Have Changed Everything

My Personal Experience
Over the Last 20 Years

There you have it. Ten tips.

I am guessing you read a few of them and immediately saw how you could integrate them into your Bible reading. (At least I hope you integrate them!) With others, you may be wondering how to apply them and what impact they will have.

Since I have been using and teaching these tips for a long time, I thought I would wrap up our time together by sharing how these tips have changed, well, everything. My approach to God's Word. My consistency in God's Word. My understanding of God's Word. My application of God's Word. And yes, my enjoyment of God's Word.

I don't want to simply reteach the tips here. *I want to show you how applying them has changed me*—and changed my experience in God's Word. Maybe the best way to show you is to look at three very different books and what I experienced as I applied the ten tips to each.

Philippians (The *First* One)

Way back in the introduction, I shared that Philippians was the first book of the Bible that I really "soaked" in. Every day. The whole summer. The whole letter each day. (Don't be too impressed. It takes only fifteen minutes to read Philippians.)

As I read Philippians over and over, it didn't take long before I started experiencing Philippians the way I would experience a letter written specifically to me. I *wanted* to read it each day. After all, if you got a letter with "I thank my God every time I remember you" as the opening line, I bet you'd read it more than once!

I started thinking about the people, the generosity of that church, the passion Paul had for Christ, and the love Paul and this church had for each other. The relationships I was seeing—between Paul, Timothy, Epaphroditus, the folks in the Philippian church, and God—caused me to think about my own relationships with God, friends, and family members.

Bottom line: For the first time in my life, I was reading the Bible relationally rather than informationally. And it was beautiful.

I would find myself thinking about the Bible throughout the day. The Holy Spirit would bring His Word to my mind at times when I needed it most. Sometimes it was a reminder that "the Lord is near" (Philippians 4), or a call to pray specifically (Philippians 1). Other times there was the question of whether there was anything I was putting above knowing Christ (Philippians 3). Occasionally, it was the not-so-gentle nudge, when my mind would go where it shouldn't, to think about what is true, noble, right, pure, etc. (Philippians 4). The Bible was more alive to me than ever before.

John (The *Longest* One)

When I started reading the gospel of John as a New Year's resolution in 1994, I had no idea God was actually preparing me for a whole new ministry! I had simply seen how amazing it was to have Philippians "in me" and wanted to know the stories of the life of Christ like I knew Philippians. I wanted to carry Him with me.

So I started reading. I didn't have the time to read the gospel of John every day. So, as I recommend at the end of Tip 4, I shifted my thinking from reading an amount of content to reading for an amount of time. Typically, I would read twenty to thirty minutes each day. Some days I would read for forty-five to sixty. Whenever I came to the end of the gospel of John, I would simply start at chapter 1 the next day. This continued for the whole year.

The concept of "watching the movie" became crystal clear for me that year. I had heard all the stories in the book of John. Most of them a bunch of times. I had read them, been taught them, heard sermons on them, and learned from them. But until 1994, I never truly had a sense of how connected they are. How much all of these stories are actually the scenes in one long movie about this guy named Jesus, who claimed to be God and saved the world!

I met Jesus in the 1970s. I fell in love with Him in 1994.

It also wasn't just Jesus I fell in love with. I started to really see—and appreciate—all of the "minor characters" in the *Big Jesus Movie*. During the years when I would simply read a chapter a day, I never noticed that Andrew and Nicodemus each show up three times. After all, several days would pass before they showed up again. Not to mention that neither of them are ever the "main character" in the stories in which they appear.

Let's focus on Andrew for a moment. I knew he was one of the disciples. I also knew he was Peter's brother. Other than that, I had never really thought about him that much. But now? He's one of my favorite people in the whole Bible. In fact, if our third child had been a boy, you would have seen the name Andrew in the dedication of this book!

I came to love Andrew only because I "watched the movie." As I became more and more familiar with the story, I noticed that he showed up in a few different places (John 1, 6, and 12). I remembered this later as I began looking more closely at the "scenes" in the movie.

Then one day, it hit me! Every time Andrew is mentioned, he's bringing someone to Jesus! How cool is that? In chapter 1, it's Peter. (That worked out pretty well, wouldn't you say?) In chapter 6, Andrew is the one who brings the little boy with a sack lunch to Jesus. (Over five thousand people surely retold that story.)

Then comes chapter 12. Jerusalem is packed for the Passover Feast. Gentiles come to Philip and tell him they'd like to see Jesus. Philip *doesn't* tell Jesus. Philip tells Andrew. And you can almost hear the unwritten conversation that follows between the two friends:

Philip: Hey, Andrew. There are all these Gentiles who want to see Jesus. But all the Jews are packed around Jesus. Jews and Gentiles! What should we do?

Andrew: Well . . . every time I bring someone to Jesus, it goes pretty well. Let's do it again and see what happens!

Can you see why I love Andrew? His default was to bring people to Jesus.

It all comes down to connections and details. Until I started reading large chunks (combined with having high expectations, reading out loud, and reading over and over), I never made the connections—I never saw how the people and events all fit together.

And I never would have appreciated so many details. I guess it shouldn't surprise me. I had experienced this truth with actual movies lots of times. Only after seeing a movie several times do we notice all the little things. These little things might not be the main point, but they make watching the movie more fun. The same is true with the Bible. Only after reading the Word several times do we start to notice—and appreciate—the little things. Even though they are not the main point, they still have much to teach us. And they add a richness and joy to reading the Bible you won't find any other way.

Jonah (The *Shortest* One)

It was the summer of 1999. My pastor and I were grabbing some lunch. He said, "I'm thinking about preaching through Jonah this fall. What do you think about kicking off the series by telling the story?" I told him I hadn't internalized Jonah yet. He said, "Hey, man, it's only two pages!" I laughed, then agreed to do it.

What happened the next several weeks was unexpected—to say the least. Now, I had started applying most of these tips six summers earlier. So I was expecting Jonah to be good. I was approaching it with a relational mindset, looking for what God had in store. I knew I would read the whole book in a single sitting. (Yes, I could pull the trigger on the eight minutes it takes to read Jonah.) I would read out loud. And I would stay in Jonah for a while, reading it each day.

But I didn't expect to be surprised. I didn't expect to discover anything new. After all, I thought I knew the story. But in reality, I really knew only 75 percent of it. That's because we typically only tell 75 percent of it. You know Jonah's story, right?

- God tells Jonah to go to Nineveh
- Jonah runs away
- Big storm
- Jonah has a three-day quiet time in the belly of a fish
- Fish vomits Jonah out (nasty!)
- God gives Jonah a second chance
- Jonah obeys (smart move)
- Ninevites repent
- God shows mercy on 120,000 people

The end. Right? *Wrong!*

That's the story I was told back in Sunday school, most likely on a flannelgraph. (By the way, if you don't know what a flannelgraph is, it means you're way younger than I am. Google it. It's Flash video for your parents' generation.) But that's Jonah 1, 2, and 3. There's a fourth chapter. And we don't tell it. Why? Because it's really bad. The book of Jonah wraps up with Jonah as a whining crybaby. Not typically the way we like to end stories.

At first I didn't like it. I wanted to go back to the familiar Jonah story. The one with the good ending. The one with the hero-obeys-and-God-saves-the-day grande finale. But that's not the way it ends. And I didn't like it, that is until I had been reading Jonah's story for about two weeks.

That is when I started realizing how kind God is for giving us chapter 4. Not only to teach us something. (Though there are lessons to learn there.) God's kindness is shown because without chapter 4, you and I would write Jonah off.

We can relate to Jonah's disobedience. We can relate to learning our lesson. And we can relate to God giving us a second chance and having God show up.

But if chapter 4 weren't there, we would see Jonah as a guy who "got it" and then rode off with God into the sunset— learned his lesson and spent the rest of his life serving God wholeheartedly, without any more slipups. We can't relate to that.

Chapter 4 reminds us that Jonah is a fickle mess. Just like you. Just like me.

Yes, those weeks with Jonah surprised me. A story I had heard so many times. A story I thought I knew. A story I thought was only about disobedience versus obedience. Little did I know it is a story about me. As I applied the tips to my time with Jonah, I was reminded—yet again—that the Living Word of God is a reality—not a phrase.

One Final Thought . . .

The books of Philippians, John, Jonah, and so many others have become dear friends over the last two decades of applying the ten tips found in this book. I believe the same thing can and will happen when you apply them.

However, after teaching these principles to thousands of people, I have one final warning: You will be tempted to ignore Tip 8 (Don't Read Alone). Don't ignore it. Please.

I have seen it over and over and over again. I believe this goes back to Tip 3 (Have a Strategy). It is one of the attacks the enemy throws at us.

Hear this clearly: You were not meant to do this alone. You will not enjoy the Bible as much as you could if you apply these tips only to your "quiet time." You will not understand the Bible as fully. You will not read it as consistently. You will not be transformed by it as completely.

Simply put, we need each other.

Nowhere have I seen this lived out so clearly as in our family's small group and in the 4-Month Bible Read Thru I have done the first four months of every year since 2010.

I can't wait to see what God has revealed to my friends. Every year I see our love for God and His Word deepen. Every year I see our enjoyment of His Word expand. Every year I want to do it again.

Apply these ten tips to your time alone in God's Word. And then, please, apply them in community.

⌘

As I type these final words, I have a smile on my face. I smile because I know the journey you are about to begin. I smile because more than twenty years ago, I was where you are. I smile because I know what is going to happen in your heart and mind over the coming weeks, months, and years. I smile because I sense God smiling over you and your time in His Word. I smile because I am confident that you are about to enjoy the Bible more than you ever dreamed possible.

Appendix A

A Small-Group Study of Ephesians

The principles of the Foundation, Framing, and Finish Work Bible-study method can be adapted very successfully for use in small groups. Naturally, a group setting brings a new dynamic to the study. In any study group, you will find some people who are committed to studying the Bible every day, while others will spend a few days a week in the Word. Still others will be brand-new to Bible study and will be just developing the habit of personal Bible study.

For most groups, a 60-Day Adventure would be overwhelming to some members of the group. You may, however, be part of a small group that desires a high level of commitment. Just make sure that you are all on the same page before beginning your study.

Following is the outline for studying Ephesians we used in our small group. Of course, the concept can be applied to any book your group chooses to study. Our group chose to have a different couple lead the discussion each week, but it would work equally well to establish a leader who would facilitate throughout the duration of the study.

Week One

The first week, commit to reading Ephesians at least four times. Some members of the group may decide to read every day, but the commitment is to a minimum of four complete readings of Ephesians.

Focus the first week's discussion on the general ideas in Ephesians—not on the specific verses. Answer questions like these: What can we learn about the relationship between Paul and the church in Ephesus from this letter? Was Paul happy with them? Frustrated? Sad? Is this an encouraging letter? What would it have felt like to receive this letter? What are the main topics?

Weeks Two and Three

During both of these weeks, continue the process of reading the entire letter to the Ephesians at least four times each week. However, what changes is the *focus of the discussions*. During week two, narrow your discussion to the first three chapters of Ephesians. Devote week three to chapters four through six. Any notes you take during your personal time should be limited to the half of the book you will be discussing the following week.

Weeks Four Through Nine

These weeks, things start to shift. The goal is to read Ephesians in its entirety *at least once* during the week. But during these weeks, you will spend most days meditating on the message of a single chapter—the same chapter each day for one week. When your group meets, share the verses, ideas, and messages that had special meaning to you. Also share the specific life applications God reveals. When you tell someone what you are going to apply, you will be much more likely to actually follow through. These focused discussions allow you to address questions you encounter in your personal study time.

Week Ten

To conclude your study in Ephesians, spend one final week discussing Ephesians as a whole. Commit once more to read Ephesians at least four times in its entirety. Talk about new insights you have gained and any questions you still have. Taking a week to simply read Ephesians again (after six weeks of digging deep) is a terrific way to end the study.

Final Thought

I highly recommend doing this with a short book of the Bible the first time. It doesn't have to be Ephesians, but don't choose anything longer than that. You will have much greater "buy in"—and "stay in"—if the daily commitment is under twenty minutes.

Obviously, since the middle weeks are focused on one chapter, the length of the study will change based on the length of the book. There will always be the first three weeks where you discuss the whole book, then the first half, then the second half. There will always be the final week when you look at the whole book again. However, while a study of Ephesians has six middle weeks, Philippians would have only four, and 1 Peter would have five.

If you already have a small group that gets together, dive on in. If not, find a few other friends, pick a book, and give it a shot.

Appendix B

A Chronological
Reading Plan

As you may know, the stories in the Bible aren't written in perfect chronological order. The primary reason is that many of the books overlap in the time periods they cover. Other books, like Psalms and Proverbs, are collections of songs, poems, and wise sayings that were written by various people who lived in different generations. Still other books, notably the writings of the prophets (Isaiah, Hosea, Jeremiah, and Ezekiel, to name a few) were written during a specific time period that is covered by as little as a couple of chapters of one of the longer historical books, like the books of Samuel, Kings, and Chronicles.

It is very helpful—and enjoyable—to read psalms, proverbs, and prophecies alongside the historical narrative that coincides with when they were written. There is no way to know the exact date when everything happened and was recorded, so different chronological Bibles will have minor variances among them. The following is a chronological reading plan I adapted from several resources, including the Blue Letter Bible, a terrific online study resource (www.blueletterbible.org), and a plan provided by the publishers of the English Standard Version of the Bible (www.esv.org/assets/pdfs/rp.chronological.pdf.). If you download the YouVersion app (free and available on every phone, tablet, and computer platform), there is a chronological reading plan built in.

The reading plan provided here will take you through the entire Bible—chronologically—in four months. Because reading for an amount of time puts you in a different mindset than reading an amount of chapters, I don't specify certain books or chapters to be read each day. Rather, I have inserted breaks as checkpoints for the end of each month so you can make sure you are not too far behind or ahead of the rest of your group. In my experience, reading through the entire Bible in four months requires a daily reading commitment of about thirty-five minutes.

The Bible in Chronological Order: A 4-Month Reading Plan

☐ Genesis 1–11
☐ Job 1–42
☐ Genesis 12–50
☐ Exodus 1–40
☐ Leviticus 1–27
☐ Numbers 1–15; Psalm 90
☐ Numbers 16–36
☐ Deuteronomy 1–34; Psalm 91
☐ Joshua 1–24
☐ Judges 1–21

End of Month One

☐ Ruth 1–4
☐ 1 Samuel 1–20; Psalms 11, 59
☐ 1 Samuel 21–24
☐ Psalms 7; 27; 31; 34; 52; 56; 120; 140–142
☐ 1 Samuel 25–27
☐ Psalms 17; 35; 54; 63
☐ 1 Samuel 28–31; Psalm 18
☐ Psalms 121; 123–125; 128–130
☐ 2 Samuel 1–4
☐ Psalms 6; 8–10; 14; 16; 19; 21
☐ 1 Chronicles 1–2
☐ Psalms 43–45; 49; 84–85; 87
☐ 1 Chronicles 3–5
☐ Psalms 73; 77–78
☐ 1 Chronicles 6
☐ Psalms 81; 88; 92–93
☐ 1 Chronicles 7–10
☐ Psalms 102–104

☐ 2 Samuel 5; 1 Chronicles 11–12
☐ Psalms 106–107; 133
☐ 1 Chronicles 13–16
☐ Psalms 1–2; 15; 22–24; 47; 68
☐ Psalms 89; 96; 100–101; 105; 132
☐ 2 Samuel 6–7; 1 Chronicles 17
☐ Psalms 25; 29; 33; 36; 39
☐ 2 Samuel 8–9; 1 Chronicles 18
☐ Psalms 50; 53; 60; 75
☐ 2 Samuel 10; 1 Chronicles 19; Psalm 20
☐ Psalms 65–67; 69–70
☐ 2 Samuel 11–12; 1 Chronicles 20
☐ Psalms 32; 51; 86; 122
☐ 2 Samuel 13–15
☐ Psalms 3–4; 12–13; 28; 55
☐ 2 Samuel 16–18
☐ Psalms 26; 40; 58; 61–62; 64
☐ 2 Samuel 19–21
☐ Psalms 5; 38; 41–42
☐ 2 Samuel 22–23; Psalms 57; 95; 97–99
☐ 2 Samuel 24; 1 Chronicles 21–22; Psalms 30; 108–110
☐ 1 Chronicles 23–25
☐ Psalms 131; 138–139; 143–145
☐ 1 Chronicles 26–29; Psalms 127; 111–118

- ☐ 1 Kings 1–2; Psalms 37; 71; 94; 119
- ☐ 1 Kings 3–4
- ☐ 2 Chronicles 1; Psalm 72
- ☐ Song of Solomon 1–8
- ☐ Proverbs 1–24
- ☐ 1 Kings 5–6; 2 Chronicles 2–3
- ☐ 1 Kings 7; 2 Chronicles 4
- ☐ 1 Kings 8; 2 Chronicles 5
- ☐ 2 Chronicles 6–7; Psalm 136
- ☐ Psalms 134; 146–150
- ☐ 1 Kings 9; 2 Chronicles 8
- ☐ Proverbs 25–29
- ☐ Ecclesiastes 1–12
- ☐ 1 Kings 10–11; 2 Chronicles 9
- ☐ Proverbs 30–31
- ☐ 1 Kings 12–14
- ☐ 2 Chronicles 10–12
- ☐ 1 Kings 15; 2 Chronicles 13–16
- ☐ 1 Kings 16; 2 Chronicles 17
- ☐ 1 Kings 17–22; 2 Chronicles 18
- ☐ 2 Chronicles 19–23
- ☐ Obadiah; Psalms 82–83

End of Month Two

- ☐ 2 Kings 1–4
- ☐ 2 Kings 5–13; 2 Chronicles 24
- ☐ 2 Kings 14; 2 Chronicles 25
- ☐ Jonah 1–4
- ☐ 2 Kings 15; 2 Chronicles 26
- ☐ Isaiah 1–8
- ☐ Amos 1–9

- ☐ 2 Chronicles 27; Isaiah 9–12
- ☐ Micah 1–7
- ☐ 2 Kings 16–17; 2 Chronicles 28
- ☐ Isaiah 13–27
- ☐ 2 Kings 18; 2 Chronicles 29–31; Psalm 48
- ☐ Hosea 1–14
- ☐ Isaiah 28–39; Psalm 76
- ☐ Isaiah 40–48
- ☐ 2 Kings 19; Psalms 46; 80; 135
- ☐ Isaiah 49–66
- ☐ 2 Kings 20–21
- ☐ 2 Chronicles 32–33
- ☐ Nahum 1–3
- ☐ 2 Kings 22–23; 2 Chronicles 34–35
- ☐ Zephaniah 1–3
- ☐ Jeremiah 1–40
- ☐ Psalms 74; 79
- ☐ 2 Kings 24–25; 2 Chronicles 36
- ☐ Habakkuk 1–3
- ☐ Jeremiah 41–52
- ☐ Lamentations 1–5
- ☐ Ezekiel 1–48
- ☐ Joel 1–3
- ☐ Daniel 1–12
- ☐ Ezra 1–6; Psalm 137
- ☐ Haggai 1–2
- ☐ Zechariah 1–14
- ☐ Esther 1–10
- ☐ Ezra 7–10
- ☐ Nehemiah 1–13; Psalm 126
- ☐ Malachi 1–4

End of Month Three

☐ Luke 1; John 1
☐ Matthew 1; Luke 2
☐ Matthew 2–3;
    Mark 1; Luke 3
☐ Matthew 4; Luke 4–5
☐ John 2–4
☐ Matthew 8; Mark 2
☐ John 5
☐ Matthew 12; Mark 3; Luke 6
☐ Matthew 5–7
☐ Matthew 9; Luke 7
☐ Matthew 11
☐ Luke 11
☐ Matthew 13; Luke 8
☐ Mark 4–5
☐ Matthew 10
☐ Matthew 14; Mark 6; Luke 9
☐ John 6
☐ Matthew 15; Mark 7
☐ Matthew 16; Mark 8
☐ Matthew 17; Mark 9
☐ Matthew 18
☐ John 7–10
☐ Luke 10–17
☐ John 11
☐ Luke 18
☐ Matthew 19; Mark 10
☐ Matthew 20–21
☐ Luke 19
☐ Mark 11; John 12
☐ Matthew 22; Mark 12

☐ Matthew 23; Luke 20–21
☐ Mark 13
☐ Matthew 24–26; Mark 14
☐ Luke 22; John 13
☐ John 14–17
☐ Matthew 27; Mark 15
☐ Luke 23; John 18–19
☐ Matthew 28; Mark 16
☐ Luke 24; John 20–21
☐ Acts 1–14
☐ James
☐ Acts 15–16
☐ Galatians
☐ Acts 17
☐ 1 and 2 Thessalonians
☐ Acts 18–19
☐ 1 and 2 Corinthians
☐ Romans
☐ Acts 20–28
☐ Colossians
☐ Philemon
☐ Ephesians
☐ Philippians
☐ 1 Timothy
☐ Titus
☐ 1 Peter
☐ Hebrews
☐ 2 Timothy
☐ 2 Peter
☐ Jude
☐ 1, 2, and 3 John
☐ Revelation 1–22

Acknowledgments

This has been such a unique and cool project. What I thought was going to be a simple, short e-book has turned into so much more. There are so many people who have either inspired this book or had a hand directly in bringing it to fruition. Thanking them all by name would take way too many pages. I am talking about a couple hundred people. Seriously.

The "Enjoy the Bible Launch Team"—I have never had a launch team before. Now I am not sure I will write another book without one. This was truly a team effort. You have read the manuscript again and again. You have found an embarrassing number of typos, grammatical errors, and places that simply needed to be cleaned up. You have provided invaluable insight on everything from the content to the study guide. The list goes on. Thank you. This has been heaps of fun!

To the readers of my blog and attendees of my presentations—You have made this book possible. You made comments on the blog, wrote me emails, shot me messages on Facebook, and spoke with me after presentations. The tips you told me were the most helpful for you are the ones found in these pages. Thank you for your encouragement to keep writing and speaking. After almost twenty years, I still love it as much as ever. More, actually.

Jeff Goins—This book is in print because of your generosity. You invited me to share the story behind an early version of these "10 Tips" on your blog. A couple of people at Bethany House read that post, reached out to me, and began the conversation that resulted in this book. I can't thank you enough for trusting me with your audience and sharing my words.

Andy McGuire—I still have the email you sent me asking if I'd be willing to explore a partnership with Bethany House. You took a risk on me. And you have been a wise, gracious guide throughout this first-timer's journey. I am deeply grateful.

Jeff Braun—It is one thing to have an editor who knows writing. It is another to have an editor who encourages, researches, challenges, and is truly a partner in the process. You are the latter. Thank you. Simply put, this book is better because of you.

Kari—It is a joy to walk this road with you. We started dating the year I was internalizing the gospel of John. We had no idea what God was up to. You were at my first presentation, only weeks before you walked down the aisle and took my name. You have walked beside me every day of this almost-two-decade journey. How about another five decades?

Sarah, Caleb, and Hannah—To see you fall more deeply in love with Jesus and His Word is truly one of the greatest joys of my life. You put up with your dad's crazy schedule with much more grace than I deserve. The best part of every trip is knowing that I get to come home to the coolest kids on the planet. And yes, we can read an extra story tonight.

About the Author

Keith Ferrin is a speaker, storyteller, and author who strives to help people realize that the living Word of God is a reality—not a phrase. He actually holds to the idea that people can believe the Bible is not only true and applicable, but also fun, engaging, and enjoyable. (Hence the reason for this book.)

He founded That You May Know Ministries in 1996 to help people fall in love with God's Word and its Author. His one-man, dramatic, word-for-word presentations of whole books of the Bible have been seen by audiences of hundreds and thousands, by young kids, college students, and (ahem) "seasoned" folks.

He is a husband to one and a father to three. And he thinks the world is a better place since the inventions of coffee and ice cream (not necessarily in that order).

Let's Connect . . .

S o, what do you think? I am genuinely interested.
There are some things I know and lots more I don't. I
need your voice. I need to hear your ideas, thoughts, struggles,
and hopes.

What are you still struggling with?

What tips would you add?

How can I serve you?

How can I serve your church, small group, or university?

What would you like to see me write about on my blog? In
my next book?

What resource would you like me to create?

There are lots of ways we can connect. Here are a few:

- Email: keith@keithferrin.com
- Blog: www.keithferrin.com

- Twitter: http://www.twitter.com/keithferrin
- Facebook: http://www.facebook.com/keithferrin

If you would like to see some clips of what I do or find out more about bringing me to your conference, university, church, or event, the best place to start is www.keithferrin.com /speaking.

Thanks for reading. Writing without reading is, well, no fun. I truly appreciate you spending your time with me. My prayer is that the next time you pick up your Bible, you will enjoy it just a little more than last time. And then a little more the next time . . . and a little more . . . and . . .

Okay . . . I think we're done. Go read your Bible. It's outstanding. Really.

Alongside,
Keith